Praise for Inquiring Minds

Minds

"With her brilliant and unique titles, her use of analogies, metaphors, real-life stories, techniques, references, and with her captivating writing and straightforward approach, Donna clearly brings the *Inquiring Minds Want to Grow* content and message home. Thought-provoking, it brings you on a journey of self-reflection and introspection, be it on a professional or personal level, equipping you with a full tool belt for growth, curiosity, self-awareness, empowerment, and so much more.

I wish I had an *Inquiring Minds Want to Grow* book when I was a young adult navigating through the, at times, bumpy and challenging corridors of life. But it's never too late, no time like the present. With insights on topics such as decoding ourselves, applying self-awareness to decision-making, to radical acceptance, this inspiring book of self-exploration and self-discovery is key—and so much fun to read! A must."

—**Dominique Denis,** B.Soc.Sc., J.D. Former RCMP & Senior Police Advisor, on a journey of discoveries in the next chapter of life.

"Just like Donna says, this book is filled with the "wait, what" snippets that transform you. It is universal and for everyone, yet still feels like it was written for your particular growth and learning. I love how each story is woven into a learning experience that gets you to self-reflect and grow."

—**Sofia Valanci**: MD PhD, Program Advisor, Learning Strategy, Royal College of Physicians and Surgeons of Canada

In *Inquiring Minds Want to Grow*, Donna Karlin gives an absolute master class on the importance of leadership, communication and asking the right questions to help us better understand ourselves, others, and navigate the world around us. For example in Chapter 16: Echoes - Making Others Feel Heard, Donna poses one simple yet very important question that all of us should keep in mind when speaking with others; "How do I want them to feel at the end of a conversation?"

There's also the "3 Second Rule, The S.T.O.P. technique" and many others which provide simple frameworks for more meaningful interactions and conversations. This book is supercharged with ideas, strategies and insights which provide all the ingredients for anyone striving to live a full and meaningful life.

—**William C. Malone**, Author: Cops in Kabul - A Newfoundland Peacekeeper in Afghanistan. Flanker Press 2018

"Donna's book *Inquiring Minds* is a masterpiece in being able to extract those ingredients in life, communication and relationships that can either sabotage us or enhance us. The essence of the book is about being able to ask powerful questions which is critical for every leader (and person) in that we have been trained instead to believe that it is all about giving advice. In reality, as Donna points out, the converse is true.

Not only does the book examine those aspects which are the keys to success such as identifying your strengths, avoiding the "shoulds" in life, knowing how to really show empathy, knowing how to effectively listen, taking the necessary risks and so on, but it ventures into that territory called the unconscious where our scripts or programming can have a very powerful impact on our lives. This is a very readable book with short punchy chapters that not only focus on a specific theme, but does so with tips and techniques embellished with real life examples. It is an invaluable addition to anyone's library in that it delves into that area of our communication and conversations called curiosity or inquiry which the majority of people really don't know how to do.

It is a book full of practical strategies based on the author's wealth of experience professionally and personally. As a leader (or anyone for that matter), this book is a must-read; it will take you to a new level in your perspective on life, and take your conversations to a new level and then ultimately, your relationships at work and elsewhere. Why wouldn't you want to obtain a copy?

  —**Dr Darryl Cross**: Leadership and Career Coach, Psychologist.
Crossways Consulting, Australia

"*Inquiring Minds* is a smorgasbord of timely, well-told stories that remind us - in so many wonderful ways - of the powers and pleasures of developing our potential. Thank you for making the time to translate you smart-earned wisdom into a fun and accessible guide for becoming a better human being - and making the world we live in and influence a better, happier, safer, and saner place."

—Dave Lent – Dave & Company: Producer, Shooter, & Editor

"Having participated in Donna Karlin's executive coaching program "Shadow Coaching®", I was extremely honored when she asked me to read an advance copy of her new book "Inquiring Minds". As I thought about it reading this book, I asked myself the questions what would I gain from reading it, was it a manual for executive coaches to use when working with their clients, was it a self-help book, or would it be a thought provoking, life changing experience?

Now having read it, I can truthfully say it is all of the above and more. It is a book that contains compassion, empathy, humor, life stories, creative, inspiration, passion and purpose. It's the exact same words that I would use to describe its author Donna Karlin. And it is definitely thought provoking and life changing – just as Donna is!

This is a book that is more than a "coaching book" although there is a great deal for coaches to learn and use when working with clients. As I read page after page, I realized Donna was taking me on a journey – a journey that would both foster and facilitate my continuing quest to be a "life-long learner". I came away feeling like I had been hugged by Donna, that she believed in me that I could be my best self, all while giving me learning opportunities as to how to look at and navigate life.

I hope you will give yourself a gift and read this book. If you do, fasten your seatbelt as Donna is about to take you on an amazing ride.

—**Lou Chrostowski**, Executive Coach and Consultant Sloan Group International

"I feel personally connected to this book, having served as Donna's co-host on Inquiring Minds, the podcast we co-created nearly four years ago. The concept of this powerful book feels like it germinated and grew out of the many fascinating and powerful conversations we've had on our show. So seeing this book come to life makes me so very proud.

As I read my advanced copy of the book, I just kept thinking about how many people it would help. Donna Karlin is a master at helping people ask the difficult, reflective questions that we all need to ask but often don't. Donna writes, "Questions serve as the tools of change, acting as our trusty flashlights and propelling us on a quest for knowledge, fueling our curiosity, and igniting mind-bending conversations. But have we fully realized the transformative might of questions?" No, Donna, we haven't, but thanks to you, we now can!

This book should be required reading for any leader. It is not a book you consume in one reading and leave on the shelf. *Inquiring Minds* has the transformative power to become a daily user manual for growing yourself and others. It will help you ask better questions, encourage deeper, more substantial conversations, and transform the way you lead. There is simply no chapter where Donna does not challenge readers to think beyond their imagination or what they've dared to consider as possible. Tap into the power of your inquiring mind and get ready, because your life and your work is about to get a whole lot more interesting."

—Steve Harper: Entrepreneur, Author, Podcaster and Chief Rippler ripplecentral.com

"Inquiring Minds Want to Grow by Donna Karlin is a compelling coaching handbook I will continuously refer to. Donna's writing style is nothing short of spellbinding, holding my attention (which is very hard to do), and creating a vivid and immersive experience for the reader. The book's pacing is impressive, taking one chapter at a time and building upon what was shared in the previous chapters. From the Illusion of Should to The Mind Maze and continuing through to Wantology, each chapter continuously challenges you to reflect by asking the right questions. Donna's artistic storytelling makes this book a standout for my personal development. Whether you've had the opportunity to be coached by Donna or not, you will appreciate the lyrical writing and a sense of fascination with growth and transforming oneself."

—Brandon Burbridge, Senior Director Global Security Solutions, Reyes Holdings

"Donna's *"Inquiring Minds"* stands out for its profound wisdom, presenting a contemporary counterpart to 'The Secret.' This impactful book not only provides a joyous learning experience but also offers invaluable insights for both personal self-reflection and professional growth, making it a comprehensive guide for navigating the challenges of today's anxiety-filled world. I love it

—**Katherine Jeans**, Producer/Director/Visual Artist

"What a concept – the power of questions and the worlds of possibility they evoke. As for curiosity, inquiry's sidekick, author Donna Karlin observes, "Embracing curiosity allows us to find grace in chaos, learning in failure, and opportunity in adversity."

Inquiring Minds offers a path for 'humans becoming,' a roadmap for spelunking oneself, observing and challenging one's self-perceptions, and reclaiming agency in generating new, stories and practices that affirm who one is and can grow into.

There is richness in every page, from the aspirational quotes to new, reframed perspectives, to tips and provocative questions that challenge one's common sense of self and expand the horizon of possibilities.

This is a book I am proud to recommend to leaders and coaches (in fact everyone) for the sake of the growth and enhanced self-leadership it promotes."

—**John Lazar**, MA, MCC, CPIF, Institute of Coaching Fellow, Founder and CEO, John B. Lazar & Associates

Inquiring Minds

Harnessing the Power of Reflective Inquiry
for Growth and Transformation

Donna Karlin

Inquiring Minds Want to Grow: Harnessing the Power of Reflective Inquiry for Growth and Transformation

First edition

ISBN: 9798385540112

Printed in the United States of America

Trademark Notice:

Shadow Coaching and Laser Coaching are registered trademarks of Donna Karlin. The use of these trademarks is strictly prohibited without the express written consent of the trademark owner.

Disclaimer:

The following disclaimer applies to the book: *Inquiring Minds Want to Grow: Harnessing the Power of Reflective Inquiry for Growth and Transformation*

1. The information contained in this book is for general informational purposes only. It is not intended as a substitute for professional advice, diagnosis, or treatment. Always seek the advice of a qualified professional regarding any specific questions or concerns you may have.

2. The author and publisher of this book have made every effort to ensure the accuracy and reliability of the information provided. However, they make no representations or warranties of any kind, express or implied, about the completeness, accuracy, reliability, suitability, or availability of the information, products, services, or related graphics contained in this book for any purpose. Any reliance you place on such information is therefore strictly at your own risk.

3. The views and opinions expressed in this book are solely those of the author and do not necessarily reflect the official policy or position of any individual, organization, or entity mentioned herein. The author and publisher are not liable for any errors or omissions, or for any loss or damage arising from the use or reliance on the information provided in this book.

4. This book may contain references or links to third-party websites or resources. These links are provided solely for convenience and informational purposes. The author and publisher do not endorse the content, products, services, or opinions expressed on any third-party websites or resources mentioned in this book. The inclusion of such links does not imply any affiliation, endorsement, or association with the linked websites or resources.

5. Every effort has been made to respect copyright laws and obtain proper permissions for the use of copyrighted material, including images, quotes, and references. If, however, any material has been inadvertently used without permission or proper attribution, the author and publisher apologize for such oversight and will rectify it in subsequent editions or reprints, upon notification.

6. The content of this book is based on the author's research, personal experiences, and observations. It is not intended to malign, defame, or harm any individual, group, or entity. Unless specified, any resemblance to actual persons, living or dead, or to real events is purely coincidental.

Disclaimer Regarding Quotes:

In the compilation of this book, every effort has been made to accurately attribute and cite all quotes to their respective sources. Multiple resources were consulted during the research and writing process to ensure the reliability of these attributions. However, despite our best efforts, errors or omissions may occur. We apologize for any unintentional inaccuracies and welcome any corrections or additional information from readers or the original sources themselves. The author and publisher take no responsibility for such errors and are committed to rectifying them in future editions, if applicable.

By reading and using the information in this book, you acknowledge that you have read, understood, and agreed to the terms of this disclaimer. If you do not agree with these terms, you should not use or rely on the information provided in this book.

Contents

This book is dedicated to the bold explorers of knowledge and transformation, who question, reflect, and seek to understand the world and themselves.

May our insatiable curiosity and courage never wane, yielding tough questions and profound insights, because an unwavering commitment to growth and self-discovery is an inspiration.

Acknowledgments

Every book is a journey, and *Inquiring Minds Want to Grow* has been no exception. This has been a journey not just of the mind and imagination, but also a collective endeavor—a coming together of many hearts and hands. As I pen these acknowledgments, a profound sense of gratitude fills me for those who have played instrumental roles in transforming this dream into reality.

I am deeply thankful for my friend Steve, whose inspiring challenge to write a book on questions I wholeheartedly embraced. Your steadfast belief in me and your encouragement to embark on this endeavor have been priceless. I am forever grateful for your unwavering support.

To my husband, Ray, you are my anchor and guide. Your patience, support, and unshakeable belief in my abilities have empowered me to persist even during the most challenging moments of writing. Your attentive ear and comforting embrace on tough days have been the invisible ink that colors every page of this book.

To my son, Michael, the beacon illuminating every word I pen. You are the inspiration behind each sentence I write. Witnessing your growth, learning, and curiosity about the world has motivated me consistently. Your enthusiasm reminds me why I undertook this journey. Thank you for embodying the inherent love for knowledge that resides within all of us.

A special acknowledgment is due to Sam Horn, my colleague, friend, and advisor. Sam, you rekindled the writer in me when the embers were fading. Your enthusiasm for the written word is contagious, and your mentorship has been a guiding light in my writing journey. Your unique blend of wisdom and wit has continually inspired me to aim higher, write better, and touch more lives. I owe you an immense debt of gratitude for pushing me to seize this incredible opportunity for personal and professional growth.

To my dedicated proofreader and editor, David Woods-Hale, and my esteemed editor, Laura E. Pasquale, my gratitude knows no bounds. Your combined efforts have given life to my book in ways I could never have achieved alone. David, your meticulous attention to detail and insightful feedback have been invaluable in perfecting every page. Laura, your expert guidance and unwavering support have transformed this creative endeavor into a profoundly transformative experience. Your collaborative spirits and steadfast commitment have left an indelible mark on this work, and for that, I extend my sincerest appreciation.

I would be remiss not to acknowledge the incredible minds whose wisdom and insights are quoted throughout this book. Their impactful words have added depth and perspective to my own, resulting in a beautiful synthesis of shared knowledge and thought. To these contributors, I express my profound gratitude. Your words have illuminated this text, infusing it with invaluable richness.

Last, my heartfelt gratitude extends to you—the reader. You are the reason these words have found a home within this book. It is my hope that *Inquiring Minds Want to Grow* serves as a catalyst for your own intellectual curiosity and contributes to your lifelong learning journey. The adage, 'It takes a village to raise a child', is invoked frequently, yet I believe it also applies to birthing a book. I extend my deepest thanks to all of you for being *my* village, for your unwavering support and contributions.

Foreword

Donna Karlin has captured her book's intent with its title. We don't just want to KNOW—we want to GROW. There's more than enough information in the world. In fact, there's a word for that. INFObesity.

The question is, what are we going to DO with all that information? How can we apply it, act on it, put it into practice? How will we use what we know to be a better leader, parent, partner?

In this inspiring book, Donna shares how we can use questions to turn monologues into dialogues so we are truly connecting on a deeper, more meaningful level. Instead of passively listening, how can we proactively leverage what we're learning—for good?

Instead of being impatient and quick to judge, how can we put our default beliefs aside and put ourselves in the other person's shoes so we're more empathetic?

Donna's original Table of Contents lets you know you're in for a delightful read. Wantology. Peeling the Psychic Onion.

The Road Less Regretted. Digging Out of a Minkhole. Behind Tinted Glasses.

You're about to have a lot of fun while getting a lot done. Be sure to have pen and paper (or your digital highlighter) handy so you can take notes on passages that resonate with you. And it's okay, even recommended, (I've checked with Donna) to underline paragraphs and dog-ear pages that are particularly relevant to you.

Socrates said, "An unexamined life is not worth living."

You're going to love the thought-provoking insights in this book that facilitate self-reflection.

You're going to love the real-life stories that put you in the scene so you can see how these techniques work in the real world.

You're going to love the specific questions provided that have the power to catalyze new insights and changed behavior— in you and in others.

You'll love how using INQUIRY can make us curious about what's happening, instead of furious about what's happening.

You'll love the action plans that show exactly how you can use these techniques in your personal and professional relationships at work, at home... even online.

Most of all, you will love Donna's humane heart which enriches these pages with her personal and professional warmth that makes you feel, seen, heard, valued and understood—and that gives you ways to make others feel seen, heard, valued and understood.

Read it and reap.

—Sam Horn, CEO of The Intrigue Agency and author of Talking on Eggshells

Preface

"It's the questions we can't answer that teach us the most. They teach us how to think. If you give a man an answer, all he gains is a little fact. But give him a question and he'll look for his own answers."

— AMERICAN AUTHOR PATRICK ROTHFUSS

One morning, while brewing a cup of insight (otherwise known as coffee), my friend Steve casually said: "I want to read your book on questions."

My confusion was evident: "What book? I haven't written a book on questions!"

His reply was both unexpected and challenging: "Well, you should! What are you waiting for?"

Such a simple notion—asking a question—can be profoundly transformative. Instead of viewing questions as mere steppingstones to answers, this book aims to elevate them to doorways of deep introspection. It's not just a collection of questions; it's a passport to the realm of reflective inquiry, inviting you to savor the journey of questioning.

Life's path is seldom a straight line; it's a labyrinth of twists, turns, and sometimes, dead ends. We all encounter instances that leave us questioning, 'Why is this happening to me?'. But what if we shift our perspective and instead ask, 'What can I learn from this?' or 'How is this situation perfect in its own way, even if it doesn't seem so?'.

Living in curiosity—residing in the question—offers us a compass through the turbulent seas of uncertainty. When we stop demanding concrete answers for every twist and turn, we free ourselves to see the perfect imperfections in our life. It's a transformative shift, allowing us to navigate complexities not as problems to be solved but as opportunities for growth and insight. Instead of being imprisoned by the 'why me?' mentality, we can open the doors to deeper understanding by asking, 'What's next?' or 'What's possible?'.

Curiosity is more than an attitude: it's a way of engaging with the world; a way of being. Embracing curiosity allows us to find grace in chaos, learning in failure, and opportunity in adversity. So, as we venture together through the intricate maze of self-perception and reflective inquiry, let curiosity be our guide. As we confront challenges, let's not seek to bypass them but to understand them, to question them, and, most importantly, to grow from them.

By adopting a posture of curiosity and inquiry, we find that life's complexities are not stumbling blocks but steppingstones on the path to transformation. And, as we delve into the power of questions, you'll see that it's not just about finding answers but about evolving in the space of not knowing, and thriving in the very questions that life presents us with.

As an accomplished Shadow Coach®, I delve into the mysterious depths of individuals' minds, helping to untangle thoughts and uncover the hidden treasures of the subconscious. Think of me less as a phantom and more as an enthusiastic tour guide armed with a flashlight.

The unanswered question is like an unopened chocolate truffle, holding tantalizing surprises within. And while a dash of cheekiness may grace these pages, don't dismiss any quips; there's often a shimmer of truth in humor.

Prepare for a transformative journey into the corners of your mind, where we'll illuminate the unseen, unearth insights, and uncover potential. Your sense of adventure will be your most valuable luggage. Armed with wit, humor, and a dash of irreverence, I'll guide you through the maze of self-perception and the art of Shadow Coaching®. We'll redefine what it means to grow and transform.

The word 'question' is much more than a tool for gaining knowledge; it's a gateway to self-discovery and reinvention.

In an interview with Oprah Winfrey in 2006, Nobel Laureate Elie Wiesel said: "In the word question, there is a beautiful word: quest. I love that word!" Wiesel's appreciation for the word 'question' as a path to self-discovery resonates with our universal quest for something more: an understanding of our identity and purpose.

Self-reflection—far from being a light snack—is a hearty meal that requires time to digest. Its power to bring about change is immense. This book offers a detour in a world addicted to instant gratification. Consider it your roadmap to self-discovery, a compass pointing towards the wisdom buried within.

The chapters that follow will explore the experience of self-discovery. We'll scrutinize societal 'shoulds', reassess our self-image, and replace narratives that no longer serve us with empowering stories. Ready to challenge the status quo? A journey of inquiry awaits, and remember, it's the questions, not the answers, that make the ride worthwhile.

Part One: The Kaleidoscope of Me

Decoding Ourselves

"The most terrifying thing is to accept oneself completely."

— FOUNDER OF ANALYTICAL PSYCHOLOGY CARL JUNG

Embarking on the journey of self-discovery is akin to navigating a labyrinth. As we confront our preconceptions and unearth the hidden gems of our identity, we can chart our destiny's course by embracing who we truly are.

Think of yourself as an explorer with your curiosity acting as a compass guiding you through the complex landscapes of self-awareness and relationships. You welcome your vulnerabilities, delve into your inner world, and awaken your dormant dreams and aspirations.

In this expedition, Laser Coaching® and Shadow Coaching® serve as specialized navigational aids. Laser Coaching®, much like a focused laser beam, swiftly zeroes in on specific roadblocks or judgments, illuminating the core issues with gentle precision. Shadow Coaching®, by contrast, dives deep into your subconscious to spotlight the overlooked elements that are vital for unlocking your full potential.

Together, these innovative coaching methodologies cut through the chaos and illusions to illuminate a path to self-acceptance. They go beyond conventional coaching techniques, revealing deeper truths and empowering you to make choices aligned with your innermost desires and values.

They encourage clients to confront their inner shadows, fostering understanding and transformative change. The courage to embrace vulnerability and dismantle self-imposed limitations leads to a personal metamorphosis, unearthing the authentic self.

Imagine a focused spotlight that harnesses your energy to unlock untapped potential, dismantle limitations, and foster empathy, compassion, and connection. This is the synergy created by Laser Coaching® and Shadow Coaching®—a dynamic duo guiding you through your mind's labyrinth to a triumphant revelation of your true self.

This transformative journey decrypts personal enigmas and sifts through layers of values and beliefs. By investigating our cultural and familial roots, our personal experiences, and the societal norms that influence us, we cultivate a deeper understanding of our identity. This exploration, marked by compassionate guidance and courageous confrontation, sets the stage for revealing our most authentic selves and deepest ambitions.

So, are you ready to ask the game-changing questions that will provoke and unveil the authentic you? Your labyrinth awaits, and the keys to navigating its twists and turns lie in the chapters ahead.

Chapter One

The Roller Coaster of Self-Exploration

"Self-transformation commences with a period of self-questioning. Questions lead to more questions, bewilderment leads to new discoveries, and growing personal awareness leads to transformation in how a person lives."

—Kilroy J. Oldster, Author

Welcome to the wild, uncharted waters of living in the questions. Jump in and join us on this electrifying exploration of our enigmatic selfhood where vulnerability, edginess, and uncharted brilliance collide.

The power of self-reflection is the power to see and transform ourselves. So, grab your metaphorical flashlight, and let's dive into the murky depths of our consciousness, seeking the shimmering treasures of insight and transformation.

Within these pages, we embark on a journey that traverses the complex landscapes of our own minds, guided by the light of introspection. As we venture deeper, we find that a faithful companion is essential for navigating the twists and turns of this expedition—a companion named self-compassion. This companion, a warm embrace for both our strengths and our vulnerabilities, is the antidote to the pressures of comparison and self-judgment. It whispers to us in moments of self-doubt, reminding us that our worth is not defined solely by accomplishments, but by our willingness to engage with life's questions authentically.

While we are all too familiar with high expectations and the fear of failure, self-compassion offers a sanctuary of self-kindness. It encourages us to treat ourselves with the same gentleness and understanding that we extend to our dearest friends. This practice, embedded in the art of self-reflection, helps us confront our imperfections with grace and curiosity rather than criticism.

With it, we learn to high-five ourselves for our awesomeness and give ourselves a comforting hug during the not-so-great moments. Forget those picture-perfect Instagram lives.

So, where do we venture first? Ah, yes—back to the conundrum that's confounded philosophers for millennia: the question, 'What makes you, you?'.

It seems simple enough, and yet this hefty question unlocks the maze of individuality and the enigma of our own unique selves, our genetic makeup, upbringing, experiences, and the cultural and societal influences that craft our identities.

As we wander through this maze, let's allow self-compassion to lead the way. This golden ticket helps us value every quirky, fun, and even clumsy aspect of ourselves. Now, as our exploration continues, let's dive into the pages of this book. We'll uncover tales of the weird, whimsical, and the 'wait, what?!' ways that self-reflection can turn our world topsy-turvy. Expect facepalms, lightbulb moments, and maybe—just maybe—a guide to becoming a smidgen better than yesterday.

The human experience is a complex tapestry woven from threads of emotion, memory, and perception. Within this intricate design are moments that defy explanation—triggers that set off emotional reactions seeming outsized compared to the situation. Whether it's the sound of someone chewing gum, the slow pace of a shopping cart, or an unexpected spoiler, these seemingly irrational triggers have an uncanny power to bring our emotions to the surface.

Hidden within these kooky triggers lies a key to unlocking deeper layers of self-awareness. The journey of self-exploration isn't merely about grand existential questions; it's also about understanding the nuances of our own emotional reactions.

Understanding these triggers is more than a curiosity—it's a vital step toward emotional intelligence. Each eyeroll or clenched jaw has a backstory scripted into the folds of our subconscious over time. These reactions might arise from childhood experiences, long-forgotten slights, or cultural imprints. Think of it as a psychological fingerprint, capturing who we are and how we navigate the world.

When we face these triggers with curiosity instead of irritation, we open ourselves to growth. We don't just identify the irritants; we probe into the 'why'. In doing so, we gain tools to navigate our emotional landscape more effectively and perhaps, those triggers may eventually lose their potency, becoming mere landmarks on our journey through the complexities of the human experience.

Pausing to examine why a simple sound or sight can ignite intense emotions reveals the complexity of our psyche. Self-reflection invites us to delve beneath the surface and ask: 'Why does this trigger affect me so strongly? What memories or associations does it evoke? What underlying beliefs contribute to my reaction?'

This exploration is like sifting through a mosaic, making sense of fragments of past experiences, beliefs, and fears. We transform seemingly irrational reactions into valuable insights. Armed with the wisdom of self-reflection, we can respond with awareness and intention the next time we encounter a trigger.

In this sense, self-exploration extends beyond grand philosophical questions to the minutiae of daily experiences. Through this deliberate examination of our reactions, we begin dismantling the walls separating us from our true selves. Shining the light of self-awareness on our triggers illuminates hidden corners of our psyche, allowing us to navigate our emotions with greater understanding and resilience. But hold on a moment—can even irrational triggers make us act unpredictably or impulsively? Yes, but self-reflection can help with that, even when dealing with life's most minuscule and pesky predicaments. The intricacies of human interactions can indeed resemble a veritable whirlwind of complexity. From the insignificant to the peculiar, let's delve into a few particularly irrational triggers that have the power to set us off, inspire a blockbuster horror movie, and even make Stephen King proud.

The Snap Crackle Pop: The sound of someone incessantly chewing or cracking their gum can ignite a fury deep within. No one quite understands why, but a fresh stick of gum can have the uncanny power to morph even the calmest person into a ticking time-bomb of stress.

Shopping Cart Escapades: An eerily familiar sense of dread envelops us when we see someone pushing their shopping cart at a snail's pace or forsaking the 'Express Lane' etiquette. Fury awaits those wanting to buy just a single bar of chocolate, trapped in an eternal queue.

Spoiler Alert Catastrophe: The moment someone carelessly disperses crucial movie or series spoilers into the unsuspecting air. There's a certain merciless satisfaction felt in knowing ahead but beware the one who spills the spoiler beans without consent—for they shall incur our wrath!

Tardy Timekeepers: Nothing makes us lose our cool quicker than someone who's consistently late and unapologetic about it. That feeling of time slipping through one's fingers, as the mind concocts wild thoughts of retribution, embodies the spirit of derangement.

Phantom Wi-Fi Woes: Is there anything more frustrating than the elusive, unreliable Wi-Fi signal? Watching the spinning circle and sporadic buffering of our favorite movie, TV show, or video induces an involuntary transformation to lunacy that rivals the finest werewolf's metamorphosis.

In one case a woman, with whom I once worked, became unhinged inexplicably by the mere sight of her boss's absurdly styled orthopedic footwear. Think Frankenstein's monster on a fashion runway. They sent her spiraling into avoidance strategies, and cringe-fests. All the while, the anxious anticipation of crossing paths with those ghastly 'sole-icitors' provoked a veritable emotional storm within her.

Puzzled by her inexplicable obsession with her boss's criminally unfashionable footwear, she mustered the courage to delve deeper. Amidst her contemplation, a thought arose: 'Could her own inner demons moonlight as cobblers in this absurd shoe drama?'

I know, my tongue-in-cheek humor might come across as irreverent, but playing with this proved to be the perfect antidote to her reaction to the situation.

She rolled up her metaphorical sleeves, grabbed the shoe by the laces, and embarked on the self-reflective voyage of a lifetime. As her mindset shifted from disdain to empathy to humor, a revelation dawned: the boss's imposing shoes might serve as a source of comfort for an undisclosed health concern, rather than simply being a fashion faux pas.

With a newfound perspective, she freed herself from the weight of emotional baggage, leaving it behind as a mere footnote in her career. She navigated the intricacies of the modern office environment gracefully, building professional rapport through careful steps and deftly maneuvering the challenges it presented.

Seems like our minds can be funny places, with molehills turning into mountains at the drop of a hat—or shoe. But here we are, navigating the zigzagging maze of life. Hats off to us, a delightfully bonkers bunch.

So, as we journey forward, let's embrace these seemingly trivial triggers as gateways to self-discovery. Through the lens of self-reflection, we transform the mundane into the profound, navigating the labyrinth of our own minds and emerging stronger, wiser, and more attuned to the subtle symphony of our emotions.

When diving into the swirling vortex of indecision, things can get... interesting. Picture the 'Promotion Promotion Predicament'. At a coaching psychology class, as I was introducing my specialized coaching techniques—Shadow Coaching® and Laser Coaching®—a young woman approached with a perplexing dilemma. She was on the verge of accepting a VP role in the pharmaceutical industry, a major leap just for her—as the first woman offered this position in her company. Impressive, right?

But beneath her composed exterior, I sensed a whirlpool of emotions. Eager to help, I delved into her narrative and asked for some background. She revealed that she, her parents, and her grandparents had lived in the city their entire lives, forming a closely-knit family unit. Similarly, her husband and his family also boasted deep roots in the same city, spanning generations. Yet, life threw a curveball—her husband snagged a promotion as well, which beckoned them to relocate across the country. This prompted me to pose three questions:

1. Would she have a job if they were to relocate, and did her company have an office in the western region to which she could transfer?

2. Were there sacrifices to be made if they moved across the country?

3. With whom did she need to have a discussion, and would she be willing to open up and share her fears, concerns, and vulnerabilities with them?

As I asked these critical questions, a smile blossomed on her face. She expressed gratitude, stating: "Until you posed these pivotal questions, I hadn't fully considered all the factors at play. I had been solely focused on the promotion itself, not even considering the significant changes it would bring to our lives.

"Even if my husband declines his promotion and we remain here, I need to evaluate whether I would get as much satisfaction from the new job as I do from my current one. The new role would require a greater emphasis on bureaucracy and less on building relationships. In addition to that, declining the promotion might have a negative impact on my future prospects within the company. I must have an open and honest conversation with my boss to address these concerns.

"And if we were to move out west, I would be left without a job, and the distance from our close-knit family, who are a critically important part of our lives, means having a heart-to-heart with my husband. Ultimately, we need to consider whether either promotion—regardless of the location—is worth the sacrifices we would have to make."

She requested some time for reflection before giving her final answers. Our conversation lasted only about 10 minutes, yet during that time, I noticed a remarkable transformation in her demeanor. She relaxed visibly, emanating a newfound sense of ease. In fact, it was the first time I had witnessed her smiling that day. By dedicating time to reflect deeply on the matter at hand, she experienced a life-altering shift.

She paused, absorbing the weight of these questions. She confessed that, while the promotion was an alluring prospect, she hadn't considered the full spectrum of its implications. There were real concerns about shifting job responsibilities, potential job loss if they moved, and the emotional distance from their families.

After some reflection, she expressed gratitude for the fresh perspective and, by the end of our brief conversation, I noticed a calm clarity in her eyes. Sometimes, even in a storm of decisions, a momentary anchor of reflection can make all the difference.

A week later, she contacted me to share their heartfelt choice: they declined both promotions and decided to remain in their cherished city. Our subsequent discussion delved deeply into self-reflection and decision-making. The essential question became, 'What should I be asking myself at this moment?'.

In retrospect, my role in that brief but transformative conversation wasn't to tell her what to do or offer solutions. Rather, it was to act as a guide, helping her laser in on the crucial questions she had been overlooking. Through Shadow Coaching® and Laser Coaching®, I aimed to shine a light on the areas that were truly essential for her—illuminating the blind spots that could otherwise have led her into an unsatisfying or compromising situation. By doing so, I equipped her with the tools to navigate her dilemma with heightened self-awareness and clarity, empowering her to make a decision that was authentically aligned with her values, priorities, and long-term goals.

This thoughtful exploration uncovered layers of considerations often overlooked in the hustle of everyday life. Guided by the beacon of introspection, we embark on life's journey, steering clear of its many pitfalls. The clarity offered by self-reflection acts as our North Star, leading us through choices that sculpt the trajectory of our futures.

And wait, there's more…

Our journey into self-reflection takes us to the radiant realm of enhanced relationships. Brace yourself for a delightful surprise: enhancing these relationships is not solely about communication (though that certainly plays a role), but also about fostering self-understanding, a key that unlocks deeper, more rewarding connections.

But that's not all. Our exploration of self-reflection extends its benefits to all types of relationships. Unraveling the intricacies of our own peculiar psyche is akin to uncovering El Dorado, a legendary city said to be teeming with gold and precious jewels, within an otherwise ordinary existence. It provides us with a reliable map for navigating the tumultuous waters of human interaction. Who would have guessed that self-understanding holds the key to excelling in the School of Social Shenanigans? It turns out that the more we know ourselves, the more proficient we become in the intricate art of conversation and companionship.

Clear and straightforward communication—even with ourselves—stands as the unsung superhero within the complex realm of relationships. Taking that brave plunge into the uncomfortable sea of vulnerability, challenging deeply ingrained beliefs, and navigating the currents of our unfiltered emotions, desires, and limitations requires a somewhat awkward yet ultimately satisfying stroke that we must all master.

Welcome to the exhilarating realm of self-discovery. Only by navigating the labyrinth of our emotions can we set up sturdy boundaries, cultivating a vibrant garden of relationships that emanates warmth and light. This process helps us cast aside the weeds and shadows, even during the coldest and most unpredictable nights.

Then there's resilience—an extraordinary ability to rebound from life's unexpected curveballs. Resilience is akin to the finesse required in crafting the perfect dish. Just as a culinary creation demands reflection on its ingredients, resilience involves contemplating difficult times and setbacks—a rising agent for personal growth. This process unveils areas for improvement, charts our course for future trials, and cultivates the mindset needed to dissect victories and failures, much like a master chef. The result? An exquisite emotional resilience soufflé, rising beautifully to every occasion.

My journey to master this complex recipe of resilience wasn't confined to coaching sessions or personal reflection. It was a journey through the crucible, where life's unexpected trials tested my limits, strength, and emotional prowess.

I recently read a LinkedIn post by organizational change management and resilience speaker Karen Ferris, that really resonated with me. She said: "Resilience is not just about bouncing back; it's about bouncing forward."

This statement served as a timely reminder, especially when I found myself facing unexpected challenges. It inspired me to take control of the chaos around me and actively shape my own life. During tough times, my family and I realized that we have the option to choose resilience.

This journey began with my confrontation with cancer. I refused to let it dominate my life's story. My dreams and passions remained intact, and I focused on what I could control, reminiscent of a chef commanding a kitchen. A few years later, our home was struck by a tornado, tearing through our lives with destructive force. Despite the turmoil, drawing from the strength forged during my battle with cancer, I weathered the storm with determination.

The tornado's impact forced us out of our house and into the process of rebuilding our lives anew. But, just as cancer's return aimed to break me, my resilience had grown stronger. With each recurrence, I anchored myself against adversity, establishing boundaries and guarding my chosen path. Amidst the tempest, I stood firm, a beacon of unwavering resilience.

In guiding others on their journeys, I employed a parallel strategy—a dance of introspection and adaptation. A trio of guiding questions formed the heart of this strategy:

'What's true?'—Or, as I like to call it, 'sifting through the sands of uncertainty'. This intriguing question beckons us to let go of preconceptions and fanciful notions, and instead seek out the solid bedrock of truths that fortify our understanding, much like a seasoned archaeologist uncovering ancient treasures buried beneath layers of shifting sands.

'What's needed?'—Just like a puzzle solver on a quest for illumination, this inquiry propels us to seek out missing pieces, confront obstacles, and explore possible avenues. Picture it as an intrepid explorer navigating a complex maze, analyzing each clue, and contemplating questions like, 'Is this indispensable?' or 'Could there be a more ingenious solution to achieve our goals with less effort?'. The pursuit of what's needed becomes a thrilling scavenger hunt, leading us closer to the enlightenment we seek.

'What's available?'—Embarking on a thrilling gastronomic journey through the abundant realm of resources is akin to a daring chef exploring a meticulously stocked pantry. Just as a seasoned epicurean, we extend our figurative culinary canvas by diligently evaluating whether we possess the essential elements; the necessary people, knowledge, time, or other vital ingredients to concoct a magnificent feast of accomplishments. If we find ourselves lacking, innovation and incremental approaches step in as the day's sous chefs, assisting us in adapting and making the most of what is at hand.

By embracing this trio, I guide others on a reflective journey of adaptation through life's ever-changing dance.

Zooming past the humdrum and diving straight into the heart of it, let's chat about the mind-bending magic of tapping into your internal chatter—yep, we're talking about that inner monologue that can thrust your life into turbo gear before you even realize it exists.

Mindful musings: Reflecting on the nitty gritty details of our thoughts decelerates them, like that time my client got super bothered by her boss's funky orthopedic shoes. One question led to another and *voilà*, the emotional uproar was defused.

Decisions, decisions: Imagine being a novice juggler, but instead of balls, you're handling life choices. It's a balancing act that meets its match with Laser Coaching®, where the

blend of swiftness and depth hits the sweet spot. Just ask
the woman torn between climbing the career ladder, trailing
her husband, or staying in her comfort zone. A life-altering
epiphany struck in just 10 minutes, and she's now grinning
like the Cheshire Cat. So, why not grapple with your own
tough choices? Ponder this: 'What outcome do I truly want,
and what am I willing to risk for it?'

Bouncing back like a rubber ball: Resilience is like a bouncy
ball—it laughs in the face of adversity's slam dunk. It goes
beyond the knee-jerk escape plan when crisis shows up;
it's about digging deep, extracting golden nuggets from
challenges, and bouncing back stronger than ever. Just like
that bouncy ball with an attitude, I've hugged resilience
tight. Battling cancer not once, but twice, turned me into a
resilience maven. Now it's part of who I am.

Stirring the creative pot: Imagine self-reflection as
your personal brainstorming bonanza, unlocking hidden
chambers of creativity you never knew existed. Ever ask
yourself so many questions you get dizzy? Well, that's
the jackpot! Unique ideas pop up, far from the same old
humdrum. It's like uncovering buried treasure by asking:
'What's true?', 'What's needed?', and 'What's available?'.

Get ready to shake hands with your wonderfully quirky self
and dive headfirst into the wild ride of self-exploration.
Let's toss perfection out the window and set off on a quest
to decode life's mysteries from the inside out. Embrace
these questions like you're embracing your favorite comfort

food—wholeheartedly and with a dash of excitement. As you do, get ready to witness the enchantment that unfolds, revealing fresh horizons and lighting up the fuse of transformation. Buckle up, because we're revving the engine of self-discovery, and it's time to let your inner brilliance dazzle the world.

Chapter Two

The Enigma of Ego Exploration

The Elusive 'Me' Conundrum

"Who in the world am I? Ah, that's the great puzzle."

—AUTHOR LEWIS CARROLL

Embarking on the thrilling, bewildering ride of personal growth, we're greeted by that weighty, age-old question: 'Who am I?'

This is the mystery of self-discovery, unearthing the vast tapestry of identity and the inexplicable power it wields. To truly uncover our inner essence, we must battle through a maze of preconceptions, societal expectations, and external influences.

Perhaps stifled by a conservative upbringing, yet guided by the hand of fate, we may discover a fervent passion for art unexpectedly. In this moment of revelation, we challenge convention and embrace our newfound artistic identity wholeheartedly.

We're a living collage of experiences—tragedies and triumphs—that morph our identities over time. And our sense of self can be as stable as a house of cards, shifting as we encounter fresh perspectives that challenge and redefine who we are. The key, though? Synchronizing our values and intending to taste that sweet authenticity.

In the labyrinth of consciousness, the cryptic riddle taunts our every waking moment, persisting into the still of the night: 'Who am I?'

This question, often confined to the realms of philosophy, spirituality, and psychology, now permeates popular discourse, inviting each of us to delve into an exploration of the ego, a journey through the elusive 'me' conundrum. As we embark on this introspective voyage, we confront a cacophony of conflicting ideas and concepts, all attempting to capture the fluid, nuanced, and paradoxical nature of the self.

"We are not one, but multitudes," poet, essayist and journalist Walt Whitman once wrote.

This phrase encapsulates the mystifying diversity of our existence. Are we simply the sum of our experiences and choices? Or are we an aggregate of personas, adapting and evolving, always striving to reconcile our internal contradictions? Is the 'me' that I perceive truly 'me'? Or is it a caricature, a self-portrait imbued with vanity and self-deception, forever trapped in the echoing hall of mirrors that is the ego?

We're not just human beings, we're humans becoming, always changing, shifting, adapting to new circumstances and challenges. This transformational aspect of our existence highlights the impermanence of self, a constant evolution often overlooked in the pursuit of a rigid, defined identity. The 'me' of yesterday is not the 'me' of today, nor the 'me' of tomorrow. Each encounter, each decision, each challenge we face molds and remolds the ever-evolving sculpture that is the self.

Our modern world, increasingly underpinned by the ubiquitous rise of artificial intelligence, adds another layer to this conundrum. If algorithms can predict our preferences, dissect our biases, and even simulate our communication styles, then what remains of the unique, the unquantifiable, the 'me'? The intersection of technology and identity erodes the bedrock of selfhood, morphing the question 'Who am I?' from an existential probe into an urgent imperative. In the face of digital echoes of our personas, maintaining an authentic sense of self has become a Herculean task.

As we unpeel the layers of the self, we confront the daunting ambiguity of personal identity. Beneath the social masks and carefully curated public personas, who are we *really*? Are we the altruists who help strangers in need or the cynics who question the strangers' motives? Are we the dreamers envisioning a utopian world or the realists grounding ourselves in harsh realities? The chameleon-like nature of the self can obscure a clear, definitive answer, further complicating our quest for self-understanding.

The exploration of ego leads us down a rabbit hole of introspection and self-analysis, but it is not an endeavor destined for futility. Rather, it is an invitation for self-transcendence; an opportunity to dismantle the fortifications of ego and uncover a more authentic, unfiltered sense of self. It urges us to discard the narrative fallacies we weave around our existence and accept the fluid, fragmented, and often paradoxical nature of our identity.

The Greek philosopher Socrates, more than two thousand years ago, advised: "Know thyself."

The wisdom of his counsel remains undiminished in our time, for within its simplicity lies the key to unraveling the paradox of ego exploration. It is not about obtaining a static, unchanging answer but about embracing the journey of self-discovery, of constantly questioning, challenging, and reinventing the 'me'.

For example, 'Maria' had always lived life by the book, obediently following the well-trodden path laid before her. Born into a family of engineers and mathematicians, she, too, found herself immersed in the world of numbers and equations, completing her degree in Mechanical Engineering, and eventually landing a respectable job at a reputable firm. On the surface, it seemed like she had it all figured out. But within her, a persistent feeling of unease gnawed at her, a sense of unfulfilled potential, an undercurrent of dissatisfaction that she couldn't quite put a finger on.

Every day on her way to work, Maria would walk past a vibrant mural—a canvas of colors and emotions that captured her city's spirit. She was mesmerized by it, drawn inexplicably to the freedom and creativity it represented. Every brushstroke on the wall resonated with a part of her that she had long suppressed.

One day, while cleaning her attic, Maria found an old box of paintbrushes and watercolors. Something stirred within her. On a whim she started to paint, clumsily at first, but with an increasing sense of joy and liberation. She discovered a part of her that reveled in the chaos of colors, the expression of emotions, and the sheer act of creating. It was as if she had unlocked a part of herself that had been sealed.

Maria began to question her identity: was she truly an engineer or an artist at heart? Could she be both? Or was she something else entirely? This newfound passion represented a stark contrast to the life she had known; the identity she had crafted meticulously. She felt torn between the security of her old identity and the exhilarating—yet terrifying—prospects of her new one.

Embracing this concept of 'humans becoming', Maria decided to embark on the journey of self-discovery. She started painting regularly, attended workshops, and even showcased her work in local exhibitions. Concurrently, she continued her day job as an engineer, discovering that the precision and analysis required in her job actually complemented her artistic pursuits, offering balance. The two aspects of her identity coexisted, each enriching the other.

Maria's story is a testament to the enigma of the ego—a poignant illustration of the elusive 'me' conundrum. Her journey underscores the truth that we are not static beings but dynamic entities, continually evolving and changing. We're not just human beings, we're humans *becoming*; always changing, shifting, adapting to new circumstances and challenges. Through her journey, Maria discovered that she wasn't solely an engineer or an artist, that she was, in fact, much more. She was a mosaic of experiences, passions, and talents, adapting continually and reshaping her identity, moving ever closer to her authentic self.

The elusive 'me' conundrum is the greatest mystery of human existence, an enigma that becomes ever more complex and fascinating with each passing moment. By leaning into its mystery, we engage in the most profound of all human endeavors: the quest for self-understanding. It is through this ceaseless exploration that we create, dismantle, and recreate the 'me', each version more refined, more authentic, and more insightful than the last. This journey, while daunting, illuminates our existence, reminding us that within the conundrum of 'me', we find the essence of humanity.

As you embark on your own exhilarating journey of self-exploration, approach it with kindness and understanding, because uncovering the authentic self can be a wonderfully messy process. Let's delve into some strategies that can help reveal our truest, most authentic self:

- Become mindful. Be here, now, and embrace practices like introspective reflection.

- Take a stroll down memory lane. Contemplate life's narrative and those pivotal moments.

- Put assumptions and beliefs under the microscope. What's really driving them? Release those that tether you to a life of conformity.

- Dive into passions and interests. Dabble in new hobbies or get back in touch with the creative self.

- Seek solitude and silence. Disconnect and tap into your inner voice.

- Allow vulnerabilities to emerge, even when it scares

the living daylights out of you.

- Practice self-compassion. Befriend fears and uncertainties—each of us is a work in progress.

This is the thrilling practice of self-exploration. Authenticity, mindfulness, self-compassion, and embracing change will be our compass as we navigate these uncharted territories.

Chapter Three

Peeling the Psychic Onion

"It's not about what you have on the outside that glitters in light, it's about what you have on the inside that shines in the dark."

—AUTHOR, POET, AND ARTIST ANTHONY LICCIONE

We are stardust seeking meaning in the vast nothingness of space, so now is the time to charge up the proton packs.

Life has an exquisitely irritating way of tossing questions at us, constantly clamoring for a response: 'Who are you? Really—who **are** you? What makes you tick, float, sink, or fly above a sea of life's choppy waters?'

There is sweet irony in spluttering without a straightforward answer to these questions. After all, we live in an age saturated with constant online personas and carefully crafted exteriors; an age in which we are nudged gently into believing that our worth is predetermined by an alluring online presence which this is, in fact, a mere façade of who we truly are.

What better place to start than to start peeling back the complex layers of the onion? The quest to solve the mystery of our identities puts us between the proverbial rock and a hard place—the forces that mold our constantly evolving sense of self.

Are you a jigsaw puzzle awaiting completion (I invite you to pick a favorite image), or a vessel adrift in stormy seas, navigating the unpredictable ocean currents?

Let us, for a moment, pretend that we are malleable clay ready to be molded by anything and everything: past experiences, expectations, societal norms, and beliefs.

While I can almost hear your inner anthropologist murmuring something about cultural factors, the ID, ego, and superego—whispering psychologist Sigmund Freud's quotes like an incantation to unlock the secret doors—the truth is that identities don't come with user manuals. Accept it. We are an inscrutable species, even to ourselves.

Having embarked on this tumultuous journey of identity exploration, don't forget that identities aren't static: they evolve, adapt, and pulse with life. Go ahead, unravel the layers, smash the fragile walls of fear and self-doubt, and relish the captivating beauty of the art that is thyself, mysterious, glittering, and impossibly complex.

In a wild world where life is an endless rollercoaster, we're all queuing for tickets to this gig called 'self-discovery'. Introspection is the new black. It's all about probing those layers of the onion—the terrain called the psyche—until our true selves emerge.

In essence, our identity suit is tailored from various layers:

- Personal: Our taste in chocolates, tendency to spout randomness, or stubbornness (thanks for that, genetics).

- Social: A mosaic of race, religion, nationality, sexuality, and more (our collective fashion statement).

- Emotional: Our rotating color wheel of moods and how we view life through those hues.

- Physical: That human wardrobe called our body, which we might appraise in the mirror.

- Cognitive: Our mind, where our various skills allow us to juggle reasoning snowballs, throw perception darts, and organize mental problem-solving carnivals.

- Spiritual: That sacred connection to the cosmic kaleidoscope (our shout-out to the universe).

- Creative: The artsy-soul food, with everything from guitar-strumming to novel-writing.

Through this funky collection of identity aspects, embracing our multiplicity brings out our genuine swagger. It's like putting on our truest shades, ready to face the world with soul-baring honesty.

Let's consider how dynamic these identity aspects really are, so dynamic that each earns its own metaphor. For instance, our personal values might sneak into our emotions, like tag-teaming wrestlers poised for the match. Or perhaps, our social identity and cognitive views do a delicate dance, interpreting the world in a way that is totally us.

Don't forget the mind-body highway, with physical and emotional identities merging like an epic crossover movie, impacting our well-being. Meanwhile, our spiritual connection serenades our personal values and purpose beautifully. Then, our creative pursuits improvise with our cognitive capabilities, jazzing up our lives and minds. It's a never-ending fiesta of connections, where we make guest appearances in all the different acts of life.

Getting to know ourselves isn't a chore. It's more like having a fun, laid-back conversation with our curiosity, high fiving ourselves for the good stuff and giving ourselves a break when we mess up. It's all about peeling back the layers, like you would with an onion, and being okay with both our wins and our quirks. We're like the stars of our own life story, embracing all our odd traits as part of our unique brand.

Delve into the depths of your eccentricities and harness their extraordinary superpowers, then raise a glass to your authentic, eccentric, and marvelous self.

Chapter Four

Flawsome Fiesta

Bloopers and Bravery with a Cheeky Grin

"It is not what you are that holds you back, it's what you think you are not."

—MOTIVATIONAL SPEAKER AND WRITER DENIS WAITLEY

Denis Waitley's musings above, strike a chord deep down in the funky core of humanity. Our messy, intricate, and brilliantly imperfect selves tend to gaze obsessively at every nook and cranny of our shortcomings. Strengths? Nah, we're too busy waltzing with self-doubt and sipping on inadequacy to notice. But what if, just for a heartbeat, we flipped the script and dared to ask, 'What awesome bits are truly worth celebrating?'.

In the labyrinth of human experience, we often find ourselves running into walls. What we fail to realize is that these barriers are often self-constructed, built from our perceived flaws rather than our strengths. But have we ever stopped to ask, 'What do I actually like about myself?'.

On our quest for self-discovery and personal growth, it's important to embark on a holistic journey that encompasses both self-appreciation and self-awareness. While reflecting on what we like about ourselves allows us to embrace our strengths and cultivate self-acceptance, it's equally valuable to acknowledge the aspects where we may fall short. As I challenge individuals to explore their self-perceived limitations, I realize the transformative power of confronting our vulnerabilities head-on.

One particular instance stands out vividly in my memory. When meeting a client for the first time, I asked a wild-card question tinged with both curiosity and purpose: 'What do you suck at?'

His face registered confusion, surprise, and a hint of discomfort. His response—'Why would you ask such a question?'—came with palpable shock. This awkward moment became a turning point, emphasizing the importance of acknowledging our self-proclaimed limitations. Confronting these perceived weaknesses can often be the first step in personal growth and transformative problem-solving.

By playfully challenging this client's self-perceptions, I noticed that he became more open and honest about his areas for improvement. Sharing these vulnerabilities led to real camaraderie and laughter. Far from becoming a liability, his authenticity acted as a catalyst for deeper connection and personal growth—both for him and those around him.

This epiphany lies at the core of embracing what I call 'flawsome': a fusion of our imperfections and strengths in a celebratory cha cha. Accepting our flawed awesomeness helps us cultivate self-compassion, frees us from the straitjacket of self-doubt, and equips us to sharpen our unique skills and gifts.

Speaking of being 'flawsome,' ever heard of Brené Brown? She's this rockstar-rific research professor and author who's pretty much the go-to person when it comes to embracing your quirks and vulnerabilities. Brené's TED Talks? Game changers. Her books? Life manuals. She dives deep into all the messy, awkward bits we usually want to sweep under the rug and says, 'Hey, these bits? They're what make you **you**.' She's the poster child for taking your so-called 'flaws' and turning them into your superpowers. Now if that's not 'flawsome,' I don't know what is.

So, how can you 'flawsomize' your life between double taps on Instagram and doomscrolling through X (previously known as Twitter)?

- Mirror Pep-Talks: Each morning, gaze into that reflection of yours and share one thing that's awesomely imperfect. Tell yourself, 'That's just flaw-some flair right there'.

- Chit-Chat Check-In: Call up a pal once a week for a 'Flawed-y Hour'. It's like Happy Hour, but you spill about quirks you're embracing instead of the latest gossip.

- Digital Detox Dance: Kick social media to the curb for an hour each day and shake your groove thing, do a little jig, or simply wiggle it out. Dance like nobody's 'gramming!

- High-Five Fiesta: As the weekend rolls in, throw a mini fiesta in your living room—yes, even if it's just you. Celebrate all the 'flawed-up' moments that led to personal wins.

- Buddy Boogie: Find a mate and become 'Imperfect Pals'. Whenever the self-doubt monster creeps in, shoot a quick text with a fun emoji or a cheeky gif. It's the perfect pick-me-up to remind you both of your fabulous 'flaw-essence'.

Feeling armed and ready to give your daily routine a 'flawsome' twist? Sweet! But you might wonder, 'Why does any of this even matter when social media keeps showing me how far I'm falling short?' Good question. Let's jump back into the messy-but-glossy world of social media and find out.

In this era where we're all glued to our screens, it's like we're bombarded by a highlight reel of other people's lives. Just flip through your phone, and it seems like everyone else is living the dream, setting this unreachable bar for the rest of us. But let's be honest. A lot of it is smoke and mirrors.

This made-up world makes us feel like we're constantly falling short, comparing ourselves to these crafted versions of reality. And who's pulling the strings? It's not just social media celebs. It's also the folks behind the ads and tech platforms. They've mastered the art of tapping into our fears and hopes, turning our insecurities into big bucks.

You're probably wondering, what's the deal with admitting we're not perfect and the whole social media comparison circus? Well, here's the tea: When we're scrolling constantly through those Insta-perfect lives, we're not just comparing our behind-the-scenes to someone else's highlight reel. We're also avoiding a face-to-face with our own not-so-glitzy moments. And let's be real, dodging those 'weak spots' keeps us stuck in a never-ending loop of self-doubt and FOMO (fear of missing out).

By acknowledging our own limitations—our 'flaws', if you will—we're taking back the steering wheel. It's like telling the world, 'Yeah, I know I'm not a master chef or a globe-trotter or a yoga guru, but that's cool because I've got my own blend of awesome'. This shift stops us from handing over our self-esteem to a bunch of strangers on the internet. When we own both our strengths and our weaknesses, we break free from that damaging need to measure up to some unattainable social media standard. And that, my friends, is what being 'flawsome' is all about.

But here's the catch: we're not just passive bystanders. We're part of the show, tossing in our own 'likes', 'comments', and 'shares', feeding this loop of self-doubt and constant comparison. Taking responsibility for that is what being 'flawsome' is all about—flawed yet awesome. It's a step towards reclaiming who we really are.

As we navigate this tricky digital landscape, let's hit the pause button now and then. Let's ask ourselves: 'Who am I, really?'

By turning our attention from what we think we're missing to who we actually are, we create a space where we can grow, accept ourselves, and feel more content.

So instead of chasing some fake idea of perfection, let's embrace our flaws and our strengths. Because these imperfections don't make us less; they fuel our growth and resilience. They make us empathetic and relatable. By doing this, we boost our self-love, equipping us to face life's ups and downs with genuine confidence.

This 'flawsome' mindset encourages us to shift from worrying about what we don't have to embracing who we are—quirks and all. We learn to team up with people who balance out our weaknesses, letting us hone what we're actually good at. We start valuing our own identity, no longer seduced by the external buzz that tries to set our worth. That way, we uncover the real gem: the power to live an authentic and fulfilling life.

Alright, team Flawsome, here's the lowdown: Life's way too short to get caught in the whirlwind of 'I wish I was...' or 'Why can't I be like...'. Forget about the flawless facades and curated lives flashing across your screen. Because guess what? You've got your own brand of magic—what I like to call 'flawsome sauce'—and that's way more important.

So go on, embrace your quirky edges, your not-so-perfect traits, and even those cringy moments you'd rather forget. They're all a part of the amazing package that is YOU. And when the world tries to tell you otherwise? Well, let's just say, the 'unfollow' button never looked so good.

Chapter Five

Identity Theft

A Metaphorical Mugging

"The greatest tragedy is to live out someone else's life thinking it was your own."

— ANGLO-IRISH POET DAVID WHYTE

Do you ever feel like life threw a surprise costume party and forgot to send you an invite? It's like you're in this maze, right? Parents, friends, 'society'—they all have opinions on who you should be. It's like carrying a rock around your neck, and let me tell you, that's not a cool accessory.

Let's take a stroll down memory lane to when I was a 16-year-old aspiring musician. My goal was a spot in a world-class orchestra through the university's rigorous music performance program. The challenges were steep, particularly for a female percussionist. Undeterred, I invested my teenage years in relentless practice. Come the audition, where my piano background and a blind judging process played to my advantage, I secured a spot in the program.

But the director had other ideas.

"You're female! You'll just get married and have kids and never go professional. I don't want to waste time on you or put you on stage," he declared.

"I'll be so good you won't have a choice but to put me on stage," I shot back.

Yup, it was my personal 'drop the mic' moment. This was just the opening act in my lifelong show of defying expectations.

Picture this: a world where we don't have to conform, where being yourself isn't just tolerated—it's celebrated! It would shake up the game, from the workplace to classrooms, all the way to Capitol Hill.

And yeah, I hear you. Too much 'me-first' thinking could turn us all into self-obsessed egomaniacs. Balance is key, right? Still, a world full of unique voices beats a sea of mindless clones any day of the week.

But let's keep it real for a sec. However, with greater freedom comes challenges—sort of like how too many cooks in a kitchen can turn a simple recipe into a hot mess. Well, if everyone's hell-bent on expressing their own unique selves, or 'doing me' as the saying goes, we might end up stepping on each other's toes—sometimes literally, sometimes not so much.

Take social media, for instance. When everyone's clamoring to show off their 'best life', it can create an unrealistic, warped perception of reality that could have us feeling inadequate.

Picture this: Sarah, a young professional, scrolls through her social media feed, bombarded with images of her peers traveling to exotic destinations, landing dream jobs, and seemingly living their best lives. As she compares her own journey to these carefully curated snapshots, self-doubt creeps in, eroding her confidence and contentment.

Or think about the workplace, where complete autonomy might mean less teamwork and collaboration.

So, the trick? Finding that sweet spot between living your best life and not getting in the way of someone else doing the same. We've got to be mindful of the community around us. It's not just about rewriting our own stories but also about being supporting characters in the lives of others.

As we each rewrite our own script, it's crazy to think about the ripple effect this could have. We're talking about shaking up stuffy old systems that thrive on us being cogs in a machine. Imagine replacing that with something that puts people first—sounds revolutionary, doesn't it?

Picture schools that celebrate what makes you, well, you. Think about TV shows and newsrooms filled with faces and stories as diverse as humanity itself. That's the kind of change we could spark.

So, what's the bottom line? It's simple. Who wouldn't want a world full of people marching to the beat of their own drum, each adding their unique flair to the mix? Trust me, the upsides are way better than any downsides.

Consider this real-world story as a testament to the transformative power of autonomy. A client of mine once dreaded going home for Christmas—something many of us can relate to. In his family home, the atmosphere was frozen in time: everyone was fixed in their pre-determined roles, regurgitating the same worn-out conversations year after year.

With resolve, he took a modest yet impactful step. He chose to sit at the back of the room, disrupting the established family dynamics. And during dinner, he opted for a different seat than his usual one. When the topic turned to his life, he seized the moment: 'By changing my physical position in this room, my perspective on our family dynamics shifted as well as did their perception of me once I filled them in on what I had accomplished.'

It was his way of sharing how he had evolved since he last lived at home.

And here's the truly remarkable part: this small change had a ripple effect. His family began to see him not as the young man they remembered, but as the adult he had become. It was as if he'd updated their understanding of who he is, simply by altering his position and speaking his authentic self into the conversation.

This heartwarming story illustrates how embracing your autonomy can lead to a profound shift in how others perceive and accept your evolving identity. By asserting his autonomy, he not only transformed his own experience but also paved the way for a more genuine connection with his family, showing that the journey to self-discovery often involves redefining our relationships with those who've known us the longest.

So, as you stand at the precipice of endless possibilities, remember that the story of your life is yours and yours alone to write. You are the author, the protagonist, and the critic—all in one. And while society may offer you a script filled with 'shoulds', 'ought-tos', and 'have-tos', it's important to ask yourself: Whose lines am I reading, and why?

Alright, so let's hit pause for a sec. Picture holding a pen in your hand, like, a magic pen that lets you draft your life's next big moves. Think about swapping out the old 'shoulds' with choices that scream '**you**'. This pen can be your ticket out of life's cookie-cutter molds and into something way more you.

Now, open your eyes and get a grip on that imaginary pen. Make a choice today that's 100% your call. It could be something tiny, like signing up for that cooking class you've been eyeing, or finally having that tough chat with someone you care about. Or hey, maybe it's choosing to binge-watch your favorite show tonight because that's what you really want.

This choice, even if it seems small, is like a stroke of ink on your life's canvas. It's your chance to say no to all the 'shoulds', 'ought-tos', and 'have-tos'. Just know that your pen's ready and itching to move to the beat of the real you.

So, what are you waiting for? Make your mark. As you do, be ready to dig into those invisible strings that seem to hold us back and start questioning why they're there in the first place. Because remember, you're the writer of your own story, and the next page is all yours to fill.

After standing my ground as a 16-year-old, defying the director's expectations, and carving my own path in the world of music, I realized the enormous power we each hold to define ourselves. That moment wasn't just a personal win; it was a turning point that underscored the importance of personal autonomy.

Your own 'drop the mic' moment is out there waiting for you, too. It begins the instant you decide to pick up the pen and become the true author of your own life story. So go ahead, make your mark—your next chapter is just waiting to be written.

Chapter Six

The Illusion of 'Should'

Ought-to's and Have-to's

"You are a unique and unrepeatable miracle of being. No one can be like you, and no one can ever take your place in the universe."

— TOLTEC SPIRITUALIST AND AUTHOR DON MIGUEL RUIZ

Have you ever been deceived by the illusion of 'should'? This sneaky snake weaves through societies, leaving vulnerable souls in the clutches of expectations not their own. Let's unmask this illusion, the ought-to's and have-to's that bind us.

Your life's remote control belongs to you, not others' notions of success or predetermined markers. By anchoring our passions to introspection, we shed light on our authentic selves, offering society's conventions a rebellious wink and striding down our uniquely mapped out road to success.

Intrigued? Let's explore life-changing tales of brave people who broke free from expectations and embraced their true selves.

Enter stage left: With few funds and my commitment to support her, a leader embarked on a transformative journey. On Day One, her leadership style revealed a combination of kindness and a fear of criticism rooted in cultural background. A thoughtful question shifted her perspective: did her team want a best friend or an inspiring mentor and leader?

This revelation ignited a wildfire within her, and she bravely faced her team. Responding to their candid feedback for stronger, more decisive leadership, they expressed a longing for a confident and empowering figure. Over the following 48 hours, she shed her outdated norms and fears, embracing a trailblazing leadership style that incorporated both empathy and authority. Her conviction strengthened; astonishing achievements followed as her team rallied under her newly invigorated guidance.

Her transformation caught the eye of the President, who promoted her to Chief of Staff 12 months later. She defied the cultural shackles that once bound her, guiding her team to new heights with authenticity. Free from societal constraints and others' expectations, her example stands as a testament to self-realization, illuminating the path for those who dare to shatter conventions and unleash their potential.

Next, meet a finance professional who believed success and financial stability were the keys to happiness. He felt like a tiny cog in a money-making machine and, as time passed, his soul withered away. He embarked on a journey of self-discovery, realizing true happiness lay outside finance.

Summoning courage, he abandoned his job and the industry to become a yoga instructor. His decision seemed foolish to others, but he couldn't continue living a life that wasn't truly his own. Two years later, his family and friends acknowledged him as a hero who followed his passion and found purpose. A dreary existence in a role that didn't interest him had been replaced by a fulfilling life as a yogi. This journey reminds us that true happiness lies in pursuing our passions and aligning our actions with our core values, values often obscured by society's obsession with money and success.

Pause for a moment and feel the exhilaration of defying 'shoulds', of moving to the beat of your heart. When we step away from the shadows of convention, we fully embrace our authentic selves, unleashing a world of limitless possibilities. Freed from the chains of societal expectations, we uncover the sheer joy of living with authenticity and passion. We dance through life, choreographing vibrant steps and making bold moves that mirror our unique essence. Guided by intuition and inner wisdom, we follow the rhythm of our hearts. With each graceful step, we nurture a deep connection with our true purpose, composing a symphony of fulfillment.

Picture a world where everybody's stuck in the same old routine, doing the same jobs, living identical lives, chasing the same goals. But hey, toss those 'shoulds' aside, and suddenly, you're the master architect of your own destiny. You start crafting roles that match your deepest desires, like deciding to become a gourmet chef when you've always loved cooking or pursuing a career in photography because capturing moments makes your heart race. And guess what? You're a unique beacon of diversity with dreams as colorful as a bag of Skittles.

Those pesky 'shoulds'? They're like wimpy puffs of smoke, easily blown away when you fan the flames of your authentic self. Maybe you're the person who starts a small business selling handmade crafts because that's where your passion truly lies, or perhaps you decide to travel the world and write about your adventures, even if everyone else thinks you should follow a traditional career path.

Stepping out of the conformity zone, you ditch the heavy coat of convention and embrace the wild freedom to explore uncharted territories. You become the trailblazer of your life, fearlessly venturing into the unknown, all driven by that insatiable curiosity and an unquenchable thirst for growth. Forget about being boxed in by other people's ideas of who you should be—you're inspired by what you can become.

But let's not kid ourselves; shaking off the 'should' illusion isn't a walk in the park. Society's got a pretty firm grip, like an overenthusiastic handshake. Yet, the treasure of unlocking your true self is right there within your reach, and a bit of self-reflection is the flashlight guiding the way. Your uniqueness shines like a neon sign in the night, carving thrilling paths that defy the norm. Success? It's no longer off-the-rack; it's tailored to fit your wildest dreams. So, what's stopping you from grabbing that toolkit and making it happen?

Time to kick those 'shoulds' to the curb and let's start painting our life's canvas with a big ol' dose of audacity, sprinkled with passion, purpose, and positivity. I mean, why settle for a bland, by-the-numbers existence when you can create a masterpiece that's uniquely you?

You see, the real treasures in life come from fully embracing yourself—the unapologetic, unfiltered, genuine YOU. You're the undisputed champion of your heart's desires, and it's about time you wore that crown proudly.

So, let's do more than just tip the scales; let's flip 'em upside down. We'll redefine success on our own terms, no more measuring up to someone else's yardstick. And when we unleash that true potential, there's no telling how high we can soar.

That whole 'Illusion of Should' thing? It's like a mirage, messing with your quest for self-discovery and happiness. As

I write this book, my journey through societal expectations becomes intertwined with the stories of those who dared to challenge it. The question, 'Who am I truly meant to be?' reverberates, urging me to explore my existence. In this quest, I unravel the stories that shaped my life. Through introspection, the deceptive nature of 'should' reveals itself.

All those expectations people pile on us are just made-up rules hiding my true self. Why should I bend over backward to meet someone else's idea of success, happiness, or fulfillment? Those chains of external expectations might be heavy, but real freedom comes from tossing them aside and deciding who I want to be.

Then, a shift occurs within me, altering my inquiry. No longer am I 'shoulding' myself to death. Instead, I ask:

- Who am I meant to be?

- How do I want to show up?

- What steps can I take to embody that?

With the burden of those imposed 'shoulds' off our shoulders, we're ready to stride down a path that celebrates our one-of-a-kind selves. We're dead set on living a life full of honesty and genuine authenticity, leaving doubt and hesitation in the dust. By embracing passion purposefully, finding our true purpose, and radiating positivity, we're not just plotting our own course but also lighting up the way for anyone who joins our journey.

Chapter Seven

"Mirror, Mirror, on the Wall"

How Do You Want to Be Seen?

"The way you show up in life will determine your success. Show up with passion, purpose, and positivity and you will be headed in the right direction."

— PRINT AND BROADCAST JOURNALIST GERMANY KENT

"Mirror, mirror, on the wall" ... or, as we call it in the 21st century, the selfie.

Being a diamond doesn't only mean being valued. In my experience, we must be willing not just to twinkle and glisten but to cut glass.

I remember learning this philosophy as a young musician. Initially, my teacher gave me as much attention as an appendix—I was unnoticed until I caused a commotion. The magic happened when sweat met skill, and when relentless perseverance pushed me into the limelight. My teacher eventually had no option but to acknowledge my talent, moving me from the wings to center stage. The new image I projected was the result of my relentless pursuit of mastery.

Charles Cooley, the American sociologist, declared: "I'm not what I think I am, and I'm not what you think I am. I am what I think you think I am."

How's that for a head-spinner?

Our self-perception is akin to a mirror that takes cues from others' viewpoints. Feedback can either polish or tarnish this mirror, significantly influencing our self-image. Cooley's wisdom also nudges us to ponder the extent to which we can or wish to manipulate the mirror's reflection to align with our desired image.

The Emergent Leader Program, a project of mine, is aimed at transforming high-potential employees who aced their roles but lacked charisma into veritable lighthouses of leadership.

One employee on the program introduced herself quietly as a "severe introvert".

With the subtlety of a sledgehammer (subtlety not being my strong suit), I asked, "Is that the image you want to project? Is that what you want everyone to remember about you?"

She admitted it wasn't, but that it was difficult to do otherwise. Her extreme shyness seemed a jarring contradiction to a regulatory role that involved holding others to account.

As we dove into the program, this young woman began to reveal a glint of passion. As we dug deeper, that ember ignited into a flame. The room fell silent as she jumped to her feet and boldly declared: "I AM THE ENFORCER!"

The transformation was shocking.

From a barely audible introduction to a full-throated proclamation, her metamorphosis was nothing short of awe-inspiring. She learned that it wasn't enough to be a crucial cog in the machine; she needed to be seen. She'd taken a journey from mouse to a lioness, revealing the true power of shaping our self-image.

At the end of the day, when she returned to her office to tidy up loose ends, her boss knocked on her door. His demeanor was a cocktail of anticipation and hesitation, as he sought to discuss the day's progress, hoping it would nurture her professional growth. Soon after their conversation, I received an enthusiastic call from him. He was as excited as a child on a rollercoaster. With a voice dipped in confidence, she had declared: "I learned that I am The Enforcer, and don't mess with me! That's my story, and I'm sticking to it!"

Her boss was as perplexed as he was intrigued about what triggered a meteoric transformation in just one day.

I nudged him to engage in a *tête-à-tête* with her. Her journey, her metamorphosis from a self-proclaimed introvert into a self-asserted Enforcer, was a story that begged to be explored. This experience birthed a consistent reminder: reflect on the seminal questions:

- Who do I appear to be to others?

- How do I show up?

It is also critical to examine our behavior under the magnifying glass, especially in challenging situations and ask:

- Am I behaving in a way that aligns with the person I aspire to be?

- Does my behavior reflect the qualities and character traits I admire and want to embody?

That young woman's story underscores the extraordinary transformative power resting within each of us. In the art of self-presentation, we sculpt others' perceptions.

The voyage of self-discovery and self-expression demands bravery, introspection, and a readiness to lock horns with our inhibitions. It's not just about changing how we're seen—it's about daring to reveal who we truly are and, in the process, becoming our best selves.

On a similar note, during another interaction with a group of women professionals, one person who had shouldered her team's responsibilities silently for years had a eureka moment. She realized she had been hampering her leadership prospects inadvertently, by enabling others' dependency. She had mistaken reliability for leadership. That day, she vowed to replace her 'doormat' label with 'leader', intent on aligning her actions with her desired image. A few months later, she couldn't wait to share that she had:

- Delved into deep self-reflection, unearthing her patterns of behavior, and taking ownership of enabling others' dependency.

- Set uncompromising boundaries that clearly defined what she was willing to do and put a stop to anything that crossed the line.

- Mastered the art of saying a resolute 'no' to tasks that didn't align with her goals or exceeded her capacity, refusing to be a pushover.

- Sharpened her assertiveness, courageously expressing her opinions and deftly negotiating like a true leader.

- Sought out trusted allies and unfiltered feedback, embracing the raw truth to fuel her transformation.

- Ignited a blazing inferno of self-confidence, celebrating her achievements, extinguishing self-doubt, and unleashing her untamed potential.

- Pursued professional development opportunities fearlessly, devouring leadership training and workshops to carve her own path.

- Sought out and conquered leadership responsibilities fiercely within her team and organization, leaving no doubt about her capability.

- Commanded the stage of communication with assertiveness and conviction, making her voice heard and respected.

- Thrived on the relentless pursuit of growth, constantly reflecting, ruthlessly identifying areas for improvement, and fearlessly adapting her approach.

From a corporate jungle to a convention, one thing is clear: being seen, and how we are seen, matters. The art of self-presentation isn't about skin-deep selfies or meticulously curated social media personas; it's about illuminating our authentic selves and unique capabilities. It's about transforming our inner 'Enforcer' or 'Leader' who refuses to be confined to the background.

As we navigate the digital realm and the relentless pressures of self-presentation, let's set aside the superficial allure of the selfie. Instead, let's direct our attention towards cultivating self-awareness, embracing authenticity, and unleashing the transformative force of self-discovery.

This is not about 'fake it 'til you make it'. This is about 'embody it 'til you become it'. We need to present ourselves in a way that aligns with who we truly want to be.

So: "Mirror, mirror, on the wall, are you ready to reflect our best selves?"

Chapter Eight

Amplified Advocacy

Using Our Voice for Maximum Impact

"Be strong enough to stand up for yourself, be yourself, and speak your truth."

—THOUGHT LEADER AND AUTHOR ROY BENNETT

Have you ever thought about just how incredibly powerful your own voice can be? I mean, *seriously*, this amazing tool can spark revolutions, change people's perspectives, and inspire a whole bunch of folks. But here's the kicker—there are all these things that often try to hush our voices.

So, if we want to unlock the full potential of our voices for making a difference, we've got to think not only about how we want others to see us but also about how we want them to hear us out. So, it's a bit like tuning a musical instrument—we want our messages to sound genuine and strike the right chords with our audience. What if your voice held the key to sparking change in your community or the world?

Just as our actions shape perceptions, the manner in which we communicate holds the key to our impact. Cultivating intentionality and mindfulness in vocal expression ensures that our messages resonate authentically and effectively with our listeners.

Think of personal expression as the path we take with our voices. When we speak sincerely, sharing our real thoughts, emotions, and experiences, it's like we're adding unique colors to the human canvas. Our individual stories? They're like powerful tools, capable of inspiring, healing, and connecting us with others in this vast world. Our words? They're like guiding lights helping others navigate the journey of life.

For instance, consider the famous 'I Have a Dream' speech by Martin Luther King Jr. His voice, exuding authenticity, resonated with millions, inspiring them to challenge racial discrimination and fight for equality. By refusing to dilute his truth, King's voice became a unique symphony, echoing with the harmonious notes of freedom, equality, and justice.

Authenticity is key, without dilution or artificial flavors. We want our voices to be as unique as a unicorn riding a skateboard, capturing the spirit of rebellion and individuality. Like a graffiti masterpiece on a bare city wall, we embrace our quirks, flaunt our flaws, and unleash our unique voice as a colorful expression that leaves an indelible mark on the world. Have you ever felt pressured to conform to societal norms? What if embracing your uniqueness could lead to meaningful change?

In a more modern context, we can take the example of Greta Thunberg, the teenage environmental activist. With her forthright speech and unyielding commitment, she moved mountains, changing public opinion, government actions, and gaining global recognition. Despite her youth, and the challenges of Asperger's Syndrome, Thunberg demonstrates the power of a confident, authentic voice, using it to drive positive change for the environment.

Empathy is more than a buzzword; it's a guiding principle that enables us to deeply understand the perspectives of those with whom we communicate. But how can we truly understand others if we don't practice empathy?

In a world often driven by division and misunderstanding, empathy serves as a bridge, allowing us to traverse the chasm that separates us from others. Have you ever wondered how understanding someone else's perspective could transform your ability to advocate for change?

First, empathy allows us to tap into the emotional and cognitive realms of others. It's one thing to assert your views loudly, but without understanding the fears, aspirations, and realities of those we wish to reach, our messages might just become noise. The true power of empathy lies in its ability to transform a monologue into a dialogue, a sermon into a conversation.

Moreover, empathy extends beyond just listening; it demands an active, intentional effort to step outside our own experiences. This often means recognizing and challenging our own biases and preconceived notions, which can cloud our understanding of the issues we're passionate about advocating. Being empathetic forces us to question these biases, to see the world through a lens other than our own.

The act of showing empathy also encourages reciprocity. When people feel heard and understood, they are more likely to extend the same courtesy to us, creating a virtuous cycle of deepening understanding. This opens doors to nuanced discussions, where diverging viewpoints can be navigated with respect rather than conflict.

And let's not forget empathy is the key to effective storytelling. When advocating for change, personal anecdotes and narratives often prove more powerful than a barrage of data and facts. Can you recall a story that profoundly influenced your beliefs or actions? What if your stories could have a similar impact on others?

In the realm of advocacy, empathy has a particular power: it allows us to find common ground in contentious or polarizing issues. When we deeply understand where someone is coming from, we are better equipped to frame our message in a way that resonates with them, creating greater potential for change. But why is empathy so pivotal, and how can we harness it to amplify our advocacy?

Consider the story of Daryl Davis, a black musician who befriended members of the Ku Klux Klan. Through genuine, empathetic conversations, he was able to sow the seeds of doubt in people who had long held racist views, leading many to renounce their ties to the Klan. This exemplifies empathy at its most transformative—the ability to foster human connections in the unlikeliest and most challenging situations, showing that even deeply ingrained prejudices can be overcome through heartfelt dialogue.

Empathy is not just an abstract ideal but a practical tool. It can be nurtured and developed, much like any other skill. Active listening, open-ended questioning, and emotional intelligence exercises are all ways to enhance our capacity for empathy.

So, as we advocate for change, let's not overlook this potent tool in our arsenal. Let's practice empathy intentionally, making it a cornerstone of our advocacy efforts. Only then can our voices truly resonate, creating echoes that inspire change across diverse communities and landscapes.

When we engage in the act of truly listening—absorbing others' words as if we were a thirsty sponge—we do more than just hear; we create a sacred space of mutual respect and understanding. In this space, our voices transcend mere noise to become harmonious melodies that resonate deeply within the souls of all who participate in the conversation.

And confidence is the secret sauce that makes our voices sing. We want our words to flow with conviction, like a politician making promises during an election campaign—minus the empty part, of course. The first obstacle to overcome is the fear of judgment, a relentless critic lurking in the shadows, waiting to pounce on our every word.

Yet, if we focus on the intrinsic value of our message and embrace authenticity as our guiding star, we can silence that judgmental beast. What if, instead of fearing judgment, we embraced the power of our own voices? It's not about applause or jeers but staying true to ourselves and letting our voices ring out.

But there's another hurdle on our path: the pressure to conform. Society often expects us to blend into the monotonous sea of sameness, but this is wrong. We can choose instead to break free from the shackles of conformity.

Another great example is that of education activist Malala Yousafzai. Facing enormous societal pressure to conform, she refused to remain silent about the importance of girls' education in her native Pakistan. Despite serious personal danger, she continued to voice her beliefs, becoming an inspiring figure, and winning the Nobel Peace Prize in the process.

In my own experience, I didn't achieve success by conforming to the same sound as everyone else in my field. Instead, my presentations aimed to shock people into awareness, encouraging them to see the entirety of their being and, at the very least, disrupt their perspective.

But there's more. Advocacy is another powerful avenue in which our voices resonate.

Consider Elie Wiesel, the renowned author and Holocaust survivor, who used his horrific experiences as a platform for advocacy against violence, repression, and racism.

His poignant writings and speeches have greatly increased awareness of these issues and inspired many to act against such atrocities. What if our voices could be the catalysts for transformative change? By using our vocal prowess to support causes aligned with our values, we can increase awareness, gather support, and spark meaningful change.

It's crucial to remember that our impact isn't dependent solely on the volume of our voice or our social status. Even in our quietest moments, we possess the power to make a difference. Change can be facilitated through the gentle flow of conversation, the written word, or acts of compassion. Engaging in heartfelt discussions, writing insightful articles and blogs, or performing small acts of kindness can create a ripple effect of goodwill, fostering unity and compassion. We don't require a grand stage or a booming voice to effect change.

Can knowledge and understanding truly be the keys to unlocking our voices? Education and enlightenment unlock doors through which our voices can enter. So, share knowledge, challenge misconceptions, and expand collective understanding. Engage in spirited discourse, teach, and write—illuminate the path towards growth, enlightenment, and progress. With this guiding torch, ignorance can be banished to the depths of a storeroom closet.

Leadership has the ability to amplify and inspire. By articulating a compelling vision, motivating others, and fostering a sense of purpose, our voices can catalyze change. Have you ever considered how your voice, like that of inspiring leaders, could motivate others to take action?

Consider the impact of voices within leadership, as exemplified by figures like Sheryl Sandberg, the past COO of Facebook. Through her book *Lean In* and numerous speeches, Sandberg has used her voice to address gender imbalance in the workplace, encourage women to assert themselves, and stimulate discussion around societal norms related to women in leadership roles. Whether it's in the professional realm, community organizations, or within our own families, our voices hold the potential to ignite passion, resilience, and transformative action.

And for those of us who are so inclined, creativity and artistry provide yet more avenues for our voices to shine. Through music, poetry, storytelling, and all forms of artistic expression, we evoke emotions, challenge societal norms, and stimulate profound introspection. Do you believe that art has the power to challenge norms and inspire conversations? What if your creative voice could be a force for change?

In that realm, we can look at artists like Lin-Manuel Miranda, creator of the hit Broadway musical *Hamilton*. By using music and storytelling, he has brought history to life, engaged millions, and opened up sensitive conversations about race, immigration, and U.S. history. His voice, through his work, is a brilliant example of how art can influence societal discourse.

After all, the most memorable symphonies are composed not of singular notes, but of diverse melodies harmoniously interwoven.

What if leadership was about inspiring through your voice, just as artists inspire through their work? Now that you've explored the potential of your voice, are you ready to use it to challenge conventions and inspire change?

Pick up your pen, your brush, and your instrument—your voice. With it, let's write a new narrative where we not only challenge conventions but shatter them, creating a world where our voices aren't just heard, but echo in the hearts and minds of others, inspiring change that reverberates through generations.

Chapter Nine

Unraveling the Narrative

The Power of Inquiry

"The value of a question isn't in the answer. It's in the exploration of the idea, the conversation that the question provokes and the journey that you go on to get to an answer."

— AUTHOR JAY BAER

In our endless quest for progress, it's high time we put the status quo on trial. Let's shine a light on the sneaky limits imposed on us by our own assumptions and biases.

Now, picture this: having the guts to question what everyone else takes for granted. It's not just about getting answers; it's about shaking up the very foundation of what we think we know. But questions are more than just curiosity—they're like fireworks, sparking vibrant discussions that light up our minds and stir our emotions, cutting through the boring weeds of convention.

So, how about we ask the ultimate question: 'What's really going on here?'

Seems simple, right? But don't be fooled. This question is the key to unlocking deep insights and breaking the chains of the status quo. 'Why bother questioning things?' you might wonder. Well, because real change, evolution, and growth can't happen if we blindly accept the same old beliefs. And on this exciting journey, we're drawn into the enchanting world of parables—a tool for enlightenment, a path to unravel the mysteries of life.

These captivating stories, packed with clever metaphors and tantalizing symbolism, challenge our thoughts, kick preconceptions to the curb, and awaken hidden truths within us. Our rebellion against the status quo takes on a new flavor, becoming a quest guided by the magic of parables, where wisdom hides in the shadows of their mysterious tales, waiting to be uncovered. Right here, at the intersection of defiance and storytelling, sparks of revolution are born, promising a brighter tomorrow.

Once upon a time, in a world not so different from ours, parables ruled as fascinating instruments of insight. These tales, wrapped in layers of metaphor and symbolism, possessed a unique magic that crossed borders and explored the depths of human thought. Parables—those timeless vessels of wisdom—appeared in diverse cultures and histories, each story a treasure trove of allegory and analogy, designed to ignite minds, inspire reflection, and light the torch of enlightenment.

These weren't just stories; they were mysterious tools passed down through generations. From the whimsical tales of Aesop to the ancient scriptures of Jesus, parables were the go-to choice for wise folks and storytellers. They held the power to puzzle, urging listeners to decipher intricate layers while stoking the fires of illumination. Through the art of storytelling, they conveyed profound truths using the language of everyday life, inviting us to explore deep ideas through familiar paths.

Metaphors and symbols, the heartbeat of parables, gave them a universal charm. They allowed messages to travel seamlessly across cultures and ages. These stories were like hidden chambers, inviting individuals to embark on journeys of interpretation, nurturing critical thinking, and sparking introspection about the very values they depicted.

Fast forward to today, and parables still shine as masterful communication tools, sources of education, and sparks for spirited conversations. They echo through time and cultures, remaining unwavering fountains of inspiration, delighting hearts, and sparking contemplation. They remind us, with a wink from their narrative eye, of the enduring power of storytelling to pass on wisdom and eternal truths.

The parable, like a crafty trickster, had the power to slip past our defenses, sneaking into our souls. It dared to hide profound truths in deceptively simple tales, spinning webs of intrigue that invited us to dig deeper and explore the hidden meanings.

With every carefully chosen word and imaginative stroke of the pen, the parable weaved its magic, drawing us into parallel worlds where universal truths danced with vivid characters and vibrant landscapes. It whispered secrets in our ears, unraveling the mysteries of existence and revealing insights that couldn't be delivered through straightforward lessons.

These tales were mirrors reflecting our deepest fears, desires, and aspirations. They held up our distorted views of reality, inviting us to question our assumptions, challenge our biases, and peer into the abyss of our souls. Through the power of the parable, we ventured into uncharted territories of thought, embracing ambiguity, complexity, and navigating the murky waters of moral dilemmas and existential questions.

In this world of imagination and metaphor, parables bridged the gap between different cultures, languages, and beliefs. Their messages transcended the confines of time and space, resonating with the human experience across generations and continents. They spoke directly to our shared humanity, reminding us that beneath our diverse exteriors, we all wrestle with the same fundamental questions and yearn for a deeper understanding of ourselves and the world around us.

But as progress marched on, the use of parables began to fade. In a world drowning in information and obsessed with instant gratification, their subtlety and nuance got drowned out by louder, more immediate forms of communication. The ancient art of storytelling—once cherished—retreated into the background as attention spans shrunk, and narratives got reduced to soundbites and tweets.

However, the power of the parable endures, calling to us from forgotten libraries and faint memories. It urges us to rekindle its transformative force. Deep within these timeless tales lie potent seeds of wisdom, waiting to be nurtured back to life.

Take, for instance, the story of a frog that lived in a well. The frog had everything he needed: water to drink, bugs to eat, and space to hop around. The well's walls kept him safe from the outside world, and he thought that was all there was to life.

One day, another animal passed by the top of the well and saw the frog inside. The animal asked the frog why he stayed in the well, and the frog replied that it was his entire world. The animal told the frog that there was a whole world outside, with many other animals, plants, and things to explore.

At first, the frog didn't believe it. But as time passed, he grew curious. He started to question his own assumptions and the limits of his world. Eventually, he summoned the courage to leap out of the well and explore the world beyond. He realized that the animal was right—there was a vast and exciting world outside the well. He was amazed by the sights and sounds, and he was grateful that he had dared to challenge his own assumptions.

The story of the frog in the well teaches us the importance of questioning the status quo and breaking out of our comfort zones. It reminds us that there's always more to learn and discover beyond our current limits. By questioning our own assumptions and facing our fears, we can achieve personal and professional growth and make the most of the opportunities that life offers.

Another way to challenge the status quo is by considering diverse perspectives. Take the story of *The Blind Men and the Elephant*, for example. Six blind men examined an elephant, each touching a different part. One thought it was like a wall, another like a spear, and so on. They all had different experiences and perceptions of the elephant. Each was correct in their own way, yet also limited by their perspective.

Transitioning from ancient parables to contemporary wisdom, we journey through the corridors of time, where storytelling has remained a constant thread weaving the tapestry of human experience. As we embrace the power of timeless narratives, we also find ourselves in the vibrant landscape of modern wisdom. Just as the ancient parables captivated minds with layers of metaphor and symbolism, there exists a TED Talk that carries the torch of enlightenment, illuminating the complexity of narratives in our interconnected world.

Delivered by the brilliant Nigerian novelist, Chimamanda Ngozi Adichie, her talk, 'The Danger of a Single Story', unfolded on the prestigious TED Global stage in 2009 in the historic city of Oxford, UK.

Adichie's narrative prowess shines through as she delves into the intricacies of our shared human experience. In her storytelling, she emphasizes that our lives and cultures are not defined by a solitary narrative but rather composed of numerous overlapping stories. She artfully illustrates how the danger of a single story lies in its potential to misrepresent the complexity of individuals, communities, and nations.

Just as the ancient parables captivated minds with layers of metaphor and symbolism, Adichie's words transcend temporal boundaries, inviting listeners to explore profound concepts through familiar avenues. Her talk becomes a modern parable, challenging us to confront the limitations of singular narratives and encouraging us to seek the richness of diverse stories.

In her passionate and authentic delivery, Adichie dismantles the notion that a single story can encapsulate the vastness of human experience. Her wisdom serves as a reminder that embracing diverse narratives is not only a matter of empathy but also a necessity to avoid critical misunderstandings. Through her narrative, she becomes a contemporary sage, offering guidance in an era where the deluge of information often obscures the nuance and depth of our shared stories. This story teaches us the importance of considering diverse viewpoints and understanding that everyone's perception of the truth can be different. It reminds us not to make assumptions based solely on our own experiences and to seek out different perspectives to broaden our understanding. By actively seeking diverse viewpoints and listening to others, we gain a more comprehensive understanding of complex issues.

Let's embrace the idea that truth is multifaceted and welcome all viewpoints into our conversations.

Chapter Ten

Provoke and Unveil

The Game-Changing Question

"With a step forward and one backward, always between yesterday and tomorrow, we live in a question without answer: does the night end or the morning begin? And if it is a day when we can change everything, why don't we see it, although our eyes are wide open?"

— ROUMANIAN AUTHOR NATASA ALINA CULEA

This quote from Romanian author Natasa Alina Culea ponders the enigmatic dance we all participate in, caught between the past and the future, always asking whether we're welcoming the dawn or saying farewell to the night. It suggests that life's most pressing questions may not have clear answers, even when we're earnestly searching for them with eyes wide open. So, what is the 'right' question in this sea of ambiguity? Who holds the compass that points to its rightness?

It's not like we're talking about an algebraic equation where the variables are known, and the result is predictable. We're into human territory here.

How do we find our footing in this quicksand of subjectivity?

Let's embark on a journey of provocation and unveiling, like an Indiana Jones of the psyche, driven to uncover not golden idols, but the shining jewel of clarity through the game-changing question.

First, it's worth noting that not all questions are created equal. There's the superficial 'How's the weather?' and then there's the soul-baring 'What's your biggest fear?'. Both serve their purpose, but only one has the power to drop a stick of dynamite into the placid lake of polite conversation. These deep, disruptive, game-changing questions disrupt equilibrium, forcing us to reassess our positions, our beliefs, our actions. Their function lies not in their shock value, but in their potential to provoke thought and, more importantly, growth.

Take, for instance, the infamous question, 'What would you do if you weren't afraid?'.

Too often, our fears are the puppet masters of our actions, turning us into marionettes dancing to the tune of trepidation. But when we're asked to visualize a reality untethered from fear, we're forced to confront the marionette strings holding us back.

Yet, provocation for provocation's sake is as useful as a chocolate teapot. The game-changing question should be strategic, carefully designed to unveil something significant. Whether it's the cloaked intention of a decision, a hidden assumption, or the unsaid truths of a relationship, the unveiling can be revelatory and transformative. In business, the question might be 'Why are we doing this the way we're doing it?'. It's deceptively simple, yet it can topple empires of conventional wisdom, and unveil new opportunities for innovation.

Or in a personal relationship, the question might be 'What are we avoiding in our conversations?'.

These game-changing questions aren't comfortable. They're not meant to be. They disrupt, provoke, and unveil to catalyze change and growth. In the intricacy of human interaction, perhaps the most daring and game-changing question is the one we are too afraid, too complacent, or too plain ignorant to ask. The pivotal question, as we've established, is an agent of disturbance, a provocateur that defies the status quo. It's worth a closer look at the reason why these questions tend to make us uncomfortable.

Why do we shy away from these questions, and why is discomfort so intrinsic to their power?

Because it is the very nature of these questions to challenge our accepted realities. They bring under the microscope the unexamined areas of our lives. More often than not, these are areas we'd rather not explore. They bring us face to face with our biases, our fears, and the comfort zones we've constructed. They break down the walls of our psychological forts and ask us to step into the unknown.

This can be unnerving. After all, we've spent years—perhaps even a lifetime—building these forts brick by painstaking brick. We've defended them from external threats, fortified them against the trials of life. And now, a single question, wielded with nothing but the sheer force of its insight, threatens to topple it all.

Take, for instance, the question, 'Why do I keep making the same mistakes?'. It's a question that forces introspection, urging us to trace the cyclical patterns of our actions and decisions. It asks us to reevaluate the beliefs that have guided these decisions, a task that can be as uncomfortable as walking barefoot on a gravel path.

It is this discomfort that is the harbinger of change. It signals the friction between old ways of thinking and the potential for new perspectives. It's a growing pain of the mind—an indication that we're stretching our boundaries of thought and reaching for a higher understanding.

Embracing the discomfort of the game-changing question can be likened to a dance. Initially, the steps may be

unfamiliar or awkward. We might stumble, might step on
a few proverbial toes. But with time, we learn to move
with the rhythm of introspection. We begin to find beauty
in the dance, the graceful pirouette of self-awareness, the
confident strut of growth.

Let's go back to our previous question in a business context:
'Why are we doing this the way we're doing it?'

The initial discomfort might stem from challenging years
of entrenched processes, defying established hierarchies,
or questioning long-held beliefs. The dance, in this case,
is about navigating the tension between tradition and
innovation, stability and disruption.

Similarly, in a personal relationship, when we ask, 'What
are we avoiding in our conversations?', we might be
unearthing delicate subjects or hidden resentments. The
dance here involves balancing truth with empathy, courage
with understanding.

Keep in mind that the game-changing question isn't a
wand to wave problems away. It doesn't promise instant
enlightenment or easy solutions. But it does promise a
dance with the truth, however uncomfortable or intricate
that dance may be. It invites us to step onto the dance floor
of introspection, to move with the rhythm of self-discovery.

What pivotal question might be asked today? It might just
end up transforming a life—your own. Perhaps the game

wasn't really about asking the right questions, but daring to face the raw, unveiled answers.

Chapter Eleven

What is the Question I Need to Ask Right Now?

"The most important questions in life can never be answered by anyone except oneself."

— ENGLISH NOVELIST JOHN FOWLES

T'was a dark and stormy night... Okay, not really, but we do all love a good cliché, don't we?

In truth, it doesn't matter what the weather was like outside the day it struck me that the single most crucial question in my life remained a mystery. You know, the big one, the question that lingers at the back of one's mind like a pesky neighbor, lying dormant in our very essence. I pondered the concept of self-discovery, of peeling back the layers of societal expectations to face the raw, unfiltered truth. Without further ado (or melodrama), I wondered:

'What is the question I need to ask right now?'

The answer to such a query, riddled with implications both subtle and profound, can elude detection like a nimble escape artist, leaving us wrestling with the shapeless void of uncertainty. Is it about love, career, or the perfect sandwich spread? Searching for that elusive question demands our wit, our courage, and our unyielding pursuit of truth.

Be forewarned: once awakened, this insatiable curiosity may just topple the very foundation of the world as you know it. But isn't that often the case when chaos births the most beautiful of awakenings?

Unearthing the perfect question in a world often bereft of sudden illumination is no less complex than navigating a labyrinth. It demands strategic thought, a descent into personal and emotional corridors, the resolve to grapple with enigmas, and a continual reframing of the discoveries within the aura of positivity.

The prize? The question that triggers conscious action, shakes the foundations of self-reflection, and illuminates the cherished treasures of life.

This beguiling question invites us to step back, to gauge our deepest priorities through the scope of each passing moment.

However, uncovering those essential questions is akin to mining for gold. Life's intricate complexities and our individual aspirations add an extra layer of difficulty to the pursuit. Here are some astute strategies to unearth the elusive treasure:

- Chart the terrain of inquiry. Pose penetrating questions like, 'What crucial aspects am I overlooking that demand attention?'.

- Observe the innermost recesses of your thoughts and emotions. Engage in debates over your values, wrestle with alternative perspectives, and chase after, 'What motivates my judgments? Are there unexplored angles to consider?'.

- Revisit past milestones and setbacks along your journey, extracting relevant questions and the elusive lessons they hold.

- Employ unexpected and unconventional methods. Begin by asking, 'What unfolds when I assume a new persona? What joys or fears lie in wait?'.

This newfound self-awareness empowers deliberate decision-making, aimed with laser precision at the heart of life's meaning.

But how do we recognize when we've struck gold? How can we identify the pivotal question? Start by examining the layers of your life as a miner inspects layers of earth.

Allow yourself the space to dig deep into your experiences and emotions. Then, go even further and ask yourself the thoughtful questions you need to hear to excavate further such as, 'What skeletons do I need to drag out from my closet for a real talk?' or 'How can I pick the lock to a new perspective when I'm stuck in a mental loop?' with the goal of unearthing the core issue.

Similar to a hidden deposit of precious metal, the answer may not be immediately apparent and may necessitate persistent effort and a willingness to break through layers of preconceived notions.

One way to foster a deep understanding of the challenges you face is by using the '5 Whys technique'. Developed by Sakichi Toyoda, the Japanese industrialist, inventor, and founder of Toyota Industries in the 1930s, this technique gained widespread recognition in the 1970s and continues to be a cornerstone of Toyota's problem-solving approach. Much like the 'go and see' philosophy upheld by Toyota, in which decisions are grounded in a comprehensive understanding of shop floor realities rather than mere boardroom speculations, the 5 Whys technique embodies a similar principle.

When applying the 5 Whys technique, you embark on a journey of inquiry by starting with a single question. Then, like following a trail of breadcrumbs, you delve progressively deeper into the layers of 'why', peeling away the layers of confusion to reveal the unvarnished truth beneath. As you persist in this quest for insight, you will gradually expose the fundamental reality at the core of the issue.

In a parallel manner, you could pause to reevaluate your progress, just as Toyota's philosophy prompts decision-makers to ask, 'What's the core question here?'.

By doing so, you not only mirror Toyota's method but also ensure your problem-solving process remains firmly anchored in the realm of genuine understanding, a philosophy that has sustained Toyota's success over the years.

For example:

Q: Why do I feel unfulfilled in my job?

A: Because I don't feel challenged enough.

Q: Why don't I feel challenged enough in my job?

A: Because I'm not using my full range of skills.

Q: Why am I not using my full range of skills?

A: Because the job description is limited, and I haven't taken the initiative to expand my role.

Q: Why haven't I taken the initiative to expand my role?

A: Because I'm afraid of stepping outside my comfort zone.

Q: Why am I afraid of stepping outside my comfort zone?

A: Because I don't want to fail or embarrass myself.

Based on this chain of questioning, the core question that needs to be addressed might be, 'How can I overcome my fear of failure and step outside my comfort zone to expand my role at work?'.

Peeling back the layers of fear and hesitation, with newfound self-awareness, we're now equipped to make decisions that truly reflect our deepest values and dreams. It's worthwhile to seek that elusive question that flips the script and incites an inner revolution. Let's dare to ask, 'What is the question I need to ask myself right now?'.

Part Two: From Mind to Matter

Applying Self-Awareness to Decision-Making

"It's not about making the right choice. It's about making a choice and making it right."

— CANADIAN AUTHOR J. R. RIM

Alright, let's shift gears as we navigate the next leg of our journey. J.R. Rim lays it out beautifully: it's not merely about making the 'right' choice; it's about owning your choice and making it work. That's the kind of wisdom that stops you in your tracks, asking you to reframe the whole way you approach decision-making.

Sound intriguing? Definitely.

In my work with clients, I dig deep into the crevices of their thought processes, dissecting how they make decisions and empowering them to take meaningful actions. It's a collaborative effort, teetering on the cusp of significant personal revelations and eye-opening insights.

In my own never-ending quest to figure out the human puzzle, I've realized something big: decisions are like the plot twists of our personal and shared life stories. They're the moments where everything can change, leaving an imprint that lasts a lifetime. But here's the kicker—many of us rush into decisions without thinking about one crucial ingredient: self-awareness.

Think of self-awareness as your personal blueprint. It encourages you to dig deep into who you are—your motivations, your biases, your emotional hot buttons. It's like having an internal GPS for your decision-making process, guiding you past the superficial stuff right into the heart of what matters.

So, let's kick routine decision-making to the curb. Instead, let's tap into the power of self-awareness to elevate our choices. By doing so, you're not just making a decision; you're making it the right one for you. It's like having your cake and eating it too—a life that's both purposeful and fulfilling. Get ready to be blown away by what you discover.

Chapter Twelve

Unleashing the Mind's Fury

Brain Excavation and Pot-Stirring Brilliance

"Asking yourself the right questions is like having a flashlight in the dark, illuminating the path ahead."

— AUTHOR AND TELEVISION HOST MEL ROBBINS

Shining a light on the darkness within ourselves is akin to being a paranormal investigator, revealing hidden mysteries lurking in the shadows. Deep within our untamed hearts lie profound truths that are much more significant than those floating on the surface of our consciousness. To uncover these elusive gems, we must embark on a wild adventure of self-interrogation.

New York Times best-selling author Mel Robbins once
compared asking the right questions to wielding a flashlight
in the dark, illuminating the path ahead. If each question
is a beam of light, then the journey of soul-searching
and contemplation becomes a dazzling spectacle—an epic
thought quest. We are not only shedding light on the path.
We are also uncovering a powerful force that breaks through
layers of bias, fear, self-doubt, and ignorance, revealing
profound truths beneath.

But what is the process of exploring the mind, and why
should we embrace it with an open mindset?

Questions serve as the tools of change, acting as our
trusty flashlights and propelling us on a quest for
knowledge, fueling our curiosity, and igniting mind-bending
conversations. But have we fully realized the transformative
might of questions?

Mind exploration is a continuous, purposeful journey. It does
not settle for the first answer that comes to mind after asking
a single question. Instead, it delves deeper, probes further,
and persistently searches for valuable insights, wisdom, and
understanding hidden beneath the surface of our thoughts.

Let's consider an example: encountering failure, a setback
that leaves you disheartened. Your initial question might
be 'Why did I fail?'. Superficial responses like 'I wasn't
adequately prepared' or 'I didn't exert enough effort', fail to
capture the whole picture.

With mind exploration, a more profound approach is employed. You begin to inquire: 'Why was I unprepared? What obstacles hindered my full commitment? What unseen challenges derailed my progress? And what can I learn from this experience?'

Each subsequent question serves as a tool for excavation, chipping away at the surface gradually, until you reach the core of your authentic self. Through this process, you unveil deeper insights into your motivations, fears, and the vast potential for personal growth that resides within you. This process is akin to embarking on an expedition of self-discovery, unearthing hidden treasures with every step of the journey.

Now, let's venture into the realm of irrational fears.

Picture this: quaking in our boots at the mere thought of public speaking seems downright ludicrous. What's the worst that could happen? We bungle a line or two—big deal! Yet, fear is common and grips like a vise. This is when the process of mind exploration unfolds like an art form. You confront your fear with a series of thoughtful inquiries: 'What makes public speaking so intimidating? What specific concerns trigger my anxiety? And why does the mere thought of these possibilities make me feel uneasy?'

As we delve deeper, we uncover layers upon layers of apprehension—concerns about embarrassment, judgment, and a persistent feeling of inadequacy. Each subsequent question acts as a gentle nudge, gradually dismantling barriers, bringing us closer to the core. Perhaps we stumble upon a childhood memory of a challenging school performance, when laughter and criticism left a lasting impression, fueling deep-seated fear of public scrutiny. Or maybe we uncover a complex tapestry of self-doubt and the pursuit of perfection, woven intricately into our being and influencing various aspects of life.

Employing the 5 Whys technique can add a bit of oomph to your excavation:

1. Why am I so afraid of public speaking?

2. Why does messing up send me into a panic?

3. Why do the audience's laughter and opinions matter?

4. Why do I let childhood echoes continue to haunt me?

5. Why do I still hold on to this outdated narrative?

By using the 5 Whys, we've unearthed a childhood memory that sparked a fear of public speaking, a fear deeply rooted in a bygone era. This newfound understanding won't make the fear evaporate instantly, but it empowers us to face it head-on, acknowledge its origins, and work tirelessly to overcome it. By shining a light on fear, we snatch away its power.

Sure, this process can be disquieting or even downright scary. But illuminating fears does not amplify them—it provides the gumption to face them. Each truth unearthed becomes a solid steppingstone on the treacherous path to kick those fears to the curb. In my Shadow/Laser Coaching®, we illuminate our darkest fears bravely, until they're no longer lurking in the shadows, ready to pounce on our dreams. By exploring the depths of our fears tirelessly, we begin to appreciate the intricate labyrinth of our psyche.

Brain excavation is a bold endeavor, much more than a mental exercise. It demands courage, resilience, and a pinch of craziness. It's a wild and daring quest for authenticity that compels us to confront and embrace our deepest selves. It pushes us to ask tough questions, grapple with uncomfortable truths, and tread fearlessly towards the precipice of the unknown. Yet, in our relentless pursuit of truth and understanding, it is an expedition we must undertake.

Socrates once declared: "The unexamined life is not worth living."

Through this daring journey, we unearth wisdom and insight that empower us to live fully, authentically, and with mischievous delight. Armed with our flashlights, pickaxes, and a devil-may-care attitude, we embark on our brain excavation adventure. The treasures we unearth will astonish, challenge, and quite possibly knock our socks off. But rest assured, they will enrich our understanding of ourselves and our place in the grand tapestry of the universe. As we dig deeper, we won't just find truths—we will find the raw, unadulterated essence of who we are.

Having delved into the profound realm of 'Brain Excavation', where we unearthed the treasures hidden within our psyche, we now turn our attention to another exhilarating endeavor: 'Stirring the Pot.'

Just as we used questions as tools to dig deep within ourselves, we will now use these very questions to disrupt complacency, challenge conventions, and ignite the flames of transformation.

If brain excavation is about deeply exploring our thoughts, stirring the pot is about injecting rebellious thinking into our minds. Both are important in our exciting journey of self-discovery and personal growth.

Computer scientist and social activist Kimberly Bryant once said: "To bring about meaningful change, we need to unleash our inner agitator armed with the power of questioning, boldness, and a commitment to real progress."

After delving into the depths of our souls and gaining new understanding, it's time to shake things up.

Stirring the pot through thought-provoking questions becomes our preferred method. It involves challenging established ideas, considering unconventional possibilities, and critically examining our own beliefs. We ask ourselves,

'What if the beliefs I hold onto are merely illusions? What if there are alternative perspectives I haven't considered? How might things unfold if I responded in a completely different way?'.

By doing this, we disrupt the settled patterns of our thinking, allowing fresh ideas and perspectives to emerge. This process goes beyond creativity; it liberates our minds. It enables us to embrace the fluidity of thought, empowering us to adapt, grow, and make better decisions in the midst of life's chaos.

As we continue our quest for self-discovery, exploring our deepest fears and uncharted beliefs, we become the architects of our minds. Through each question, examination, and stirring, we shape and reshape the landscapes within us. It's an active engagement with our inner selves, a journey that confirms our capacity for limitless growth and transformative change.

To those who boldly refuse to conform, who challenge the status quo with a mischievous smile, and who ignite the flames of change fearlessly: rejoice! Unleash your inner agitator, armed not with a mere utensil, but with the most powerful tool of all: thought-provoking questions that cut through complacency, ignite deep thinking, and fuel progress.

In a world suffocating under the weight of comfort and conformity, it is the relentless agitators who rise above the ordinary. They reject things that are ordinary, unimpressive, or lacking in substance and choose to challenge the foundations of complacency. They question what is considered unquestionable and push the boundaries of what is deemed acceptable. With a spark of mischief in their eyes, they stir the pot with fervor, daring to disrupt the monotony and spark transformative change.

Equipped with their arsenal of questions, they break down the barriers that confine us. They open minds, dismantling apathy, and nurturing a thirst for knowledge and change. Undeterred by the pressure to conform, they understand that progress stems from the discomfort of unsettled thoughts.

And speaking of stirring the pot, I have a story to share. It happened at the 2016 TED Women Conference in San Francisco where a colleague was helping me put together my profile. She looked at me with a mischievous grin and said: "You, my friend, are a true pot stirrer."

I was taken aback for a moment, assuming she meant it as a negative remark. But she quickly clarified that "…being a pot stirrer is a compliment. It means you're not afraid to challenge the status quo, to ask the tough questions, and to shake things up. It means you're willing to disrupt the norm and ignite change".

Her words resonated with me deeply. I realized that being a pot stirrer is not about creating chaos for the sake of chaos.

It is about pushing boundaries, challenging assumptions, and sparking conversations that lead to transformation. It is about infusing thought with a hint of rebellious rebellion, churning our collective consciousness to provoke new ideas and perspectives.

Since that day, I have embraced the title of 'pot stirrer' with pride. I've continued to ask the tough questions, to question the unquestionable, and to encourage others to do the same. And I've seen the incredible power that stirring the pot can have in our personal growth and in driving meaningful change in the world.

So, let's continue on our journey as pot stirrers. Let's wield our questions like stirring spoons, creating ripples that disrupt complacency and spark innovation. Let's challenge the status quo, embrace discomfort, and fearlessly explore the boundaries of our beliefs, ignite the fires of change, and unleash a world of endless possibilities.

Chapter Thirteen

Behind Tinted Glasses

Delving into the Heart of Bias

"Let's invite one another in. Maybe then we can begin to fear less, to make fewer wrong assumptions, to let go of the biases and stereotypes that unnecessarily divide us."

—FORMER FIRST LADY OF THE UNITED STATES MICHELLE OBAMA

The carousel of curiosity spins endlessly, driven by an insatiable yearning for knowledge. It embraces every experience—but biases cast a shadow, distorting its journey. With mindful introspection, we can navigate through these obstacles, allowing the carousel to spin freely, revealing a clearer perspective. The carousel of curiosity must confront biases persistently, ensuring its pursuit of knowledge remains vibrant and unhindered.

To see with crystalline clarity, we must banish the spectacles of prejudice. To listen with truth, we must drown out the hiss of stereotype static. And to love with depth, we must wrap our arms around our shared humanity in its messy and brilliant spectacle.

Biases are the ghostly goggles that tint our reality and warp our cognition. They are the offspring of our past encounters, cultural upbringing, social mingling, and even our brain's sneaky shortcuts. These biases can nestle deep within us, steering our actions and interactions surreptitiously in ways we might barely grasp. This subtle operation of biases is aptly illustrated in the timeless fable *The Fox and the Grapes*.

This tale recounts the experience of a fox encountering a vineyard where it spies a cluster of grapes hanging high on a vine. Eager to savor the luscious fruit, the fox makes numerous attempts to leap and seize the grapes, but unhappily, falls short each time. Frustrated and defeated, the fox resigns, departing with a muttered proclamation: "Those grapes were probably sour anyway."

This fable serves as a poignant reminder of how our biases can lead us to belittle or distrust something, merely because it eludes our grasp. The fox, unable to attain the grapes, fabricates a narrative that the grapes themselves are unworthy or inferior, rather than acknowledging its own limitations.

This story challenges us to question our own biases and assumptions, and to avoid dismissing something out of hand simply because we cannot immediately attain it. It reminds us that our biases and expectations can color our perception of reality, so we must work actively to overcome them in order to truly see the world as it is. We all have biases, beliefs, and assumptions that we hold without even realizing it. When we examine our own biases, we can question the assumptions that underlie the status quo and challenge ourselves to see things in a new light.

We've poked the hornet's nest. We've defied our beliefs. We've ruffled the status quo's feathers. And in doing so, we've caught fleeting glimpses of our inner rebel. The next stage in our expedition isn't a mere step, but a daring vault, an ambitious leap towards unmasking the biases that suffocate authentic connections, illuminated by the wisdom of former US First Lady Michelle Obama, who, in her 2018 book *Becoming,* wrote: "There's power in allowing yourself to be known and heard, in owning your unique story, in using your authentic voice. And there's grace in being willing to know and hear others. This, for me, is how we become."

Our conscious and unconscious biases are like tinted sunglasses, colorizing our perceptions and sculpting our interactions. These shades—much like the layers of dust on a vintage photo—blur the real image. They skew our understanding, fog our verdicts, and erect an invisible barrier between us and others. But what if we could buff those shades to transparency? What if we could behold the world, and each other, with virgin, unbiased eyes?

Debiasing isn't about suppressing differences or denying our past experiences. It's about acknowledging these differences, deciphering their origins, and then putting our assumptions on trial. It's about recognizing that our individual experiences and backgrounds are the lens through which we view the world, but they need not restrict our vision.

Biases are like silent puppeteers that entwine their strings in our relationships. They can strangle authenticity by nurturing misunderstandings, snaring our judgement, and stifling empathy. They can blind us from truly seeing others while keeping us tied to the narrow confines of our preconceived notions.

In one workshop, I delved into the pervasive biases that hinder genuine connections. I designed an exercise aimed at confronting participants with their own biases. They could not anticipate the unexpected manner in which I would challenge their preconceived notions.

I kicked things off by handing out unique numbers to each participant—a sort of badge of honor, if you will. This numbering system wasn't just about maintaining order; it was a mirror reflecting the biases we unwittingly cradle while establishing connections. Each number was a window into someone's world.

I asked participants to consider, despite not knowing each other, who they would choose as their dream partner and whom they would rather avoid. It was a gutsy task, forcing everyone to face their own assumptions and snap judgments right in the eye.

Picture the big reveal: the pairings were out, and the room was buzzing with a mix of shock and intrigue. Believe it or not, most people found themselves paired up with folks they didn't even consider as partners— a surprise twist, thanks to a random algorithm at play. The tension in the room was electric as everyone tried to wrap their heads around these unexpected partnerships. And guess what? I saved the kicker for the end of the first day—that whole randomness thing? Yep, it was all part of the plan. The goal was to shake things up, challenge assumptions, and pave the way for real, authentic connections.

As the day unfolded, the participants engaged in conversations and activities with their unexpected partners. They unearthed shared passions, surprising commonalities, and unique perspectives they had missed before. Slowly but surely, the fortress of bias started to crumble, replaced by a budding curiosity and a growing desire to see beyond superficial judgements.

The exercise was more than a lesson; it was a metamorphosis. It revealed the potency of challenging our biases and re-evaluating our preconceptions. It emphasized that to truly connect with others in a sincere and meaningful way, we must first scrub our lenses clean of these biases. The challenge resided in learning to pause, question, and reassess.

Debiasing is about making this practice second nature—the mental gymnastics we perform consistently, not just in our personal interactions but also in our wider understanding of the world. It's about actively striving to shatter stereotypes, rise above prejudices and misconceptions, and embrace the shared human experience in all its magnificent diversity.

Debiasing, though, is only half the battle. The other half is about substituting these biases with understanding, empathy, and genuine connection. It's about "inviting one another in", as Michelle Obama puts it, and staying open to knowing and hearing others. It's about appreciating our shared human attributes, our universal battles and victories, and our mutual longing for acceptance and belonging.

So, are you ready to leap? Ready to challenge your biases? Ready to reveal your blind spots? Ready to invite one another in?

The way to do all of this is through a voyage of constant questioning and self-correction, a journey that promises the beauty of shared experiences, the power of authentic relationships, and the transformative potential of unfiltered understanding.

Chapter Fourteen

Reflect to Connect

The Power of Self-Awareness in Relationships

"A great relationship is about two things: first, appreciating the similarities, and second, respecting the differences."

— MOTIVATIONAL SPEAKER AND AUTHOR TOMER YOGEV

Imagine a seasoned hiker preparing for a daunting, yet beautiful journey. Their backpack is full, but their most essential tool is intangible: their innate self-awareness. This is akin to our journey on the relationship highway, a dynamic panorama of human connections ranging from familial to romantic ties.

Navigating this diverse terrain requires a unique kind of GPS: Grounded Personal Self-awareness.

Deep self-understanding, which is at the core of the intriguing mirror effect of self-reflection in relationships. The mirror effect, a captivating phenomenon that has piqued the interest of influential psychologists throughout history, is an enlightening metaphor. It places us in front of our own reflections, illuminating the interconnectedness between our self-perception and the dynamics within our relationships. Every interaction becomes a mirror reflecting the depths of our inner world.

Our relationships act as echoes of this internal world. In essence, every connection we form serves as a mirror reflecting aspects of our own identity, beliefs, and emotions. As aptly noted by motivational speaker and author Tomer Yogev, a healthy and wholesome relationship not only celebrates shared interests but also acknowledges and respects differences. Therefore, when we say, 'Our relationships echo this inner world, each connection a mirror', we mean that the way we relate to others often reveals facets of our own personality and worldview. Just like a mirror reflects our external appearance, our relationships mirror our internal landscape.

Consider Alice and Bob, lifelong friends with contrasting personalities. Alice, a bookworm, thrives in solitude and has an intense passion for literature. She often loses herself in the thrilling works of Stephen King. On the other hand, Bob, a social butterfly, enjoys bustling social scenes and escapes reality through J.K. Rowling's magical narratives.

They've remained friends for decades, navigating through the ebbs and flows of their lives. Their shared love for literature has been a common thread, bridging their contrasting personalities. However, their differences are also stark. Alice prefers quiet corners and introspective discussions about the deeper themes and psychological aspects of the books they read. Bob, however, thrives in the energetic ambiance of book launches and literature festivals, engaging in animated debates about the fantastical elements in their shared reading experiences.

Their enduring friendship exemplifies Yogev's principle: Bob and Alice celebrate their common ground while also acknowledging and respecting their differences. They understand that their dissimilar preferences in social settings do not hinder their connection but instead enrich it, providing balance and breadth to their perspectives.

Inevitably, like in any relationship, disagreements arise. For example, they once had a heated debate about their favorite authors. Alice couldn't understand Bob's fascination with Rowling's wizarding world, while Bob couldn't grasp Alice's attraction to King's horror stories. The disagreement escalated, their mirror cracked, and distorted reflections of themselves and each other took over.

However, their self-awareness and the principles of the mirror effect came to their rescue. They stepped back, reflecting on their emotions and reactions. Alice sought to understand Bob's love for the extraordinary world of Harry

Potter, and Bob attempted to appreciate Alice's interest in the psychological complexity of King's characters. They listened to one another, not to respond, but to understand each other's perspective.

In the end, they reconciled, not because they shared the same favorite author, but because they respected their own individual differences. Their mirror mended, reflecting a deeper understanding of each other and a stronger bond. Their story showcases how Yogev's principle, and the mirror effect can help to navigate the complex terrain of interpersonal relationships, even amidst conflict.

Navigating this terrain requires us to have the humility to acknowledge when we've reacted based on biases or misunderstandings. It demands that we put aside our egos and truly listen to the perspectives of others, even when they challenge our own beliefs. Yet, the benefits are profound. Self-awareness fosters open communication, empathy, and trust. It allows us to take responsibility for our actions and reactions, leading to more constructive conflict resolution. When we're self-aware, we can identify patterns in our behavior and work towards breaking negative cycles.

As we merge onto the enthralling relationship highway, the mirror effect illuminates not only our path but ourselves; it helps us recognize our blind spots, shortcomings, and biases, all potential roadblocks on our journey. Armed with this understanding, we can transform challenges into chances for self-improvement.

The mirror effect transcends traditional introspection. It's not just about self-contemplation in solitude, but about reflecting on our actions and responses within our relationships. Each interaction is an opportunity to look into the mirror and thus, into our selves. This reflection fosters empathy and strengthens our bonds with others.

To revisit Yogev's words: "A great relationship is about two things: First, appreciating the similarities, and second, respecting the differences."

With the mirror effect, we add a third: reflecting to connect, honoring the power of self-awareness in every interaction we have.

In the end, self-awareness doesn't merely enhance our relationships; it transforms them into journeys of discovery and growth. 'Reflect to connect' is more than a mantra; it's the map for navigating the relationship highway. Listening with bias is like looking into a foggy mirror; the fog of preconceptions blurs the reflection, obstructing understanding.

To clear away the fog of preconceptions, we can use some practical tools in our daily lives. Here are a few everyday hacks for the eager 'reflectors' among us:

1. **Ink Therapy:** Get scribbling. Ink Therapy encourages you to grab that pen or fire up your keyboard and dive into the labyrinth of your emotions and thoughts. Let your words flow as

you navigate the twists and turns, revealing both hidden treasures and lurking monsters within. This therapeutic form of self-expression is your ticket to self-discovery, where the act of writing becomes a mirror reflecting your innermost self. It's not about perfection but embracing vulnerability, granting you the freedom to process, understand, and embrace your complexities. Unleash your thoughts, explore your feelings, and take charge of your narrative—Ink Therapy is your guide on this introspective adventure.

2. **Time Travel / Stay in the Now:** Where the practice of mindfulness and meditation becomes your relationship yoga—strengthening emotional flexibility, balance, and resilience. As you step away from the past's worries and the future's anxieties, mindfulness becomes your time machine, rooting you in the present, fostering a deeper connection with yourself and those around you. Meanwhile, meditation serves as your tranquil oasis, cultivating focus and emotional well-being, allowing you to respond thoughtfully to the dynamic tapestry of relationships. Just as yoga nurtures physical flexibility, these practices grant emotional adaptability, while the strength you gain is the emotional resilience needed to navigate the challenges and uncertainties relationships bring. Embrace this journey, and watch yourself transform

into a more poised, centered, and emotionally empowered individual within the intricate web of connections.

3. **Sound Check:** Dive into the realm of self-awareness and self-reflection through the captivating concept of 'Sound Check'. Imagine tuning into your personal feedback station, where you attune yourself to the subtler frequencies of your thoughts, emotions, and interactions. As you listen closely, you'll uncover hidden melodies and insightful harmonies that might have eluded your awareness. Just as tuning a radio reveals previously unheard music, this practice enables you to catch the golden tunes of self-discovery, offering a chance to embrace facets of yourself that may have remained unexplored amidst the noise of everyday life.

4. **Book a Date with Yourself:** Who better to hang out with than your own charming self? Indulge in the delightful notion of 'Booking a Date with Yourself', a cherished opportunity to spend quality time with your most captivating companion—you! Picture setting aside dedicated moments free from distractions, where you can engage in introspection and self-discovery. Just as sharing time with a dear friend allows for meaningful conversations, this self-date offers a chance to reflect deeply, nurturing a dialogue with your thoughts, dreams,

and aspirations. Amidst the hustle and bustle of
life, this tranquil rendezvous becomes a sanctuary
of self-care, nurturing the bond with your own
thoughts, and fostering a profound connection that
enriches your relationship with others as well.

5. **Ear Hustling:** Sharpen those listening skills. Instead
of thinking up witty comebacks while the other
person is still talking, give them your full attention.
By truly focusing on their words, you'll unveil a
world of insights that might have otherwise slipped
through the cracks. This practice transforms your
interactions into meaningful exchanges, where you
absorb nuances and emotions that might have
gone unnoticed. Just as a keen observer captures
intricate details in a painting, you'll be astonished
by the depth and richness of the conversations
you've been missing out on while lost in your own
thoughts. This exercise enriches your connections,
allowing you to forge more genuine bonds by being
present and receptive, and opening the door to
profound understandings you might have otherwise
overlooked in the rush of daily life.

6. **Shoe Shuffle:** Embrace the whimsical act of 'Shoe
Shuffle', a dance that encourages you to step
into another's shoes and sway to their rhythm.
By immersing yourself in their perspective, you
cultivate a potent dose of empathy that not only

fosters a profound connection but also unveils hidden insights and shared humanity. This dance of understanding enriches your interactions, weaving threads of compassion and understanding that strengthen the tapestry of relationships. Just as trying on different shoes offers new perspectives on comfort and style, embracing empathy reveals the harmonious steps of your own unique journey, while also amplifying the harmony you create with others in this intricate dance of life.

Sprinkle these hacks into your daily routine, and you'll soon see your mirror shine brighter, reflecting clearer images of yourself and those around you.

It's important to recognize that self-awareness practices may vary across cultures and contexts. Different cultures may have varying norms around introspection, emotional expression, and relationship dynamics. Consider how cultural factors influence self-awareness and adapt your approach accordingly. Additionally, take into account the context of the relationship. For example, a professional relationship may require a different level of self-awareness than an intimate partnership.

Remember, self-awareness is like a road trip in that it's more about the journey than the destination. Every day brings a fresh opportunity to tune-up the engine, clear the windscreen, and cruise down the relationship highway with a bit more style and confidence. Every interaction is an opportunity; a mirror that reflects a part of us. So buckle up and get ready to cruise down this highway of self-discovery and stronger connections.

Chapter Fifteen

Beneath the Surface

Listening to Understand, Not to Judge

"If you understand others, you are smart. If you understand yourself, you are illuminated. If you overcome others, you are powerful. If you overcome yourself, you have strength."

— CHINESE TAOIST PHILOSOPHER LAO TZU

Ever wonder if, in our ceaseless yammering, we're just broadcasting judgment or thirsting to fathom the depths of others' thoughts? Humanity's chatter hides a vital, customarily disregarded skill, both a balm to fractured hearts and a bridge across the chasms of our souls: the art of listening.

One may deem listening to be a passive undertaking, but beyond this façade lurks a vigorous fusion of heart and mind. In Adam Kahane's literary marvel *Solving Tough Problems*

(2007), we're struck by the kind of listening that leaves one feeling stark naked in the face of a conversation, void of assumptions, ready to be clothed by the wisdom of others.

Eavesdropping on the soul doesn't mean just sponging the words and ideas of others; it demands ditching our preconceptions, pausing our assessments, and diving head-first into the unknown seas of different lives lived. In a world riddled with schisms, sometimes the wise opt to listen, balancing on the knife-edge of understanding and judgment.

As someone who works in the realm of human growth, I can't help but relish the metamorphic power that listening holds. We live in an age of fleeting soundbites and pithy tweets, our ears craving the tones of human connection more than ever. Judgment lurks like quicksand, beckoning us to make snap calls based on scant knowledge and prejudices.

To cultivate true understanding and engage in meaningful conversations, it is crucial to ask ourselves a series of thought-provoking questions. Consider the following:

- When we strip away our assumptions, who's the person we're really talking to? It helps us put our biases on the backburner and get to know others as they are.

- Are we just waiting to say our piece, or are we actually trying to get what the other person is saying? Sometimes, we're so eager to chime in that we miss the point.

- What kind of vibes are hiding behind those words? Conversations are like icebergs; there's often a lot more beneath the surface.

- Ever thought about the 'music' in conversations? They've got their own rhythm and flow. Are we tuning in, or just hearing the words?

- Are we quick to judge, or are we taking the time to figure things out? We all tend to jump to conclusions, but slowing down can lead to better understanding.

- How do these words hit us, deep down? Our reactions and feelings are part of the chat. Understanding them can make the conversation richer.

- What assumptions are we sneakily making? It's normal to make guesses, but pausing to question them can open doors to deeper insights.

- What if we threw in a few more questions? The right ones can make the conversation way more interesting and clear things up.

Embracing these reflective questions propels us into mental acrobatics, bouncing between assumptions and understanding, grasping the essence of empathetic listening. Let's embark on this journey of silent eloquence, where understanding blossoms in the pauses between words. Through genuinely listening, may we comprehend more than we judge, connect more than we divide, and illuminate rather than casting shadows.

To sharpen our listening tools, we must first confront our own reflections: biases, preconceptions, and our penchant for conclusions. Sure, the mind adores labeling things and putting them in boxes but grasping anything of real import requires a ravenous curiosity that questions everything.

Kahane proposes that, through reflective questions and deep listening, we transform ourselves and our interactions. It's like trading myopic lenses for kaleidoscopes, thereby enriching us, and making space for heartfelt exchanges.

Imagine two politically opposed people. A masterful listener wouldn't dismiss the other as a muddle-headed buffoon but seek the roots of what has nourished their ideology. In doing so, they might unveil a shared passion for community welfare, blooming from disparate seeds of their worldviews. Now, that's true conversational alchemy.

For instance, during a TED talk at the 2019 TED Summit in Edinburgh, Scotland, journalist Jochen Wegner shared an intriguing story about an audacious project. This unique initiative brought together more than 17,000 strangers from 33 different nations, connecting them for political discussions. It was almost like Tinder, the popular dating app, but with a twist. This audacious project played matchmaker for political adversaries in a kind of tinderbox Tinder.

Wegner, the mastermind behind these conversational blind dates, revealed that these daring *tête-à-têtes* sparked more than just heated debates. In fact, together they became an intriguing experiment on how the lost art of face-to-face conversation could reignite our empathy and help mend a fractured world.

Heeding the call to truly listen—and not to judge—demands restraint, humility, and a feverish thirst for moving past the superficial. This means casting ego aside to bask in the sunshine of human experience; silencing judgment in favor of curiosity and empathy. In this space, authentic dialogue thrives, and we're reminded that even the most discordant notes contribute to the grandeur of our shared masterpiece.

To sum up: To listen is to play mental hopscotch across the chasms dividing us, arms outstretched. By truly listening, we can metamorphose the pursuit of validation, control, and purpose into playful human connection.

Ready to crack open the shell of old assumptions and dive deep into the sea of empathetic listening? Then let's carry forward one final reflective question: 'How does listening invite the wisdom and insights of others to help untangle our own challenges?'

This question recognizes the transformative power of collective wisdom, paving the way for future conversations on interdependent problem-solving. Together, we are not solitary islands but terrain that strengthens and enhances the whole.

Chapter Sixteen

Echoes

Making Others Feel Heard

"Listening is a magnetic and strange thing, a creative force. The friends who listen to us are the ones we move toward. When we are listened to, it creates us, makes us unfold and expand."

—AUTHOR BRENDA UELAND

'How do I want them to feel at the end of the conversation?'

This is a question I often reflect on, a clever technique to prioritize listening over speaking and add a touch of wonder to the dialogue.

How about we dive into the anatomy of a great conversation? Let's start with active listening.

It's like a mixtape of techniques that really set the stage for awesome conversations. Picture it this way: paraphrasing is like taking that awesome tune you just heard and playing it back in your own style. It's like saying, 'Hey, I'm right there with you, and I totally get what you're sharing.' And those open-ended questions? They're like the crescendo of the track, encouraging the speaker to keep the jam going and share their whole story.

Building on the concept of active listening, one of the ways I stay centered on any conversation is by applying what I call the 3-Second Rule. This is more than just a catchy phrase; it's a practice of allowing three full seconds to pass in silence after the other person has finished speaking. These three tiny ticks of the clock create a space that lets your conversational partner feel not just heard, but also deeply considered.

Now, let's take the 3-Second Rule a step further. Imagine for a moment that each conversation you have is akin to creating a work of art. Think about that time you sat with your best friend at a coffee shop. Every brushstroke was a sentence as you wove the vibrant tapestry of gossip, musings, and shared dreams.

Every hue hidden in that tapestry was an emotion—unspoken, but palpable. When your friend shared their anxieties about changing jobs, you didn't just nod along; you gave space for that story to take shape, contouring the colors and providing a frame of understanding. And what was the result? A masterpiece of dialogue, that's what. You both walked away feeling like

Picasso on a good day—or at the very least like two people who genuinely got each other.

However, even the most artistically crafted conversation can be ruined by a common foe: multitasking. Have you ever tried cooking pasta, petting your dog, and genuinely engaging with a heartfelt story from your friend while furiously thumbing through emails on your phones? Spoiler alert: The pasta will be overcooked, your dog confused, and your friend feeling like they just talked to a wall.

Multitasking is the sworn nemesis of active listening, the villain in our well-intended tale of meaningful conversations. We think we're being efficient, but let's be honest, we're more like scatterbrained octopuses than adept jugglers. We all do it, but the next time you catch yourself multitasking during a conversation, remember to S.T.O.P.

- Stop what you're doing.

- Take a few deep breaths.

- Observe your surroundings, and then

- Proceed with the conversation. This mindfulness technique can quickly bring you back to the present moment.

Speaking of obstacles, let's bring up those little gremlins we call biases—the preconceptions and assumptions that worm their way into conversations uninvited. You think you already know what your neighbor is going to complain about when she starts with her, "You won't believe what happened today!".

Maybe you do, maybe you don't. But the trick? Hit the mental pause button and wipe that mental slate clean for a minute.

Give her your full, unadulterated attention. Or employ a technique known as Reflective Listening. This involves actively summarizing what the other person has said or asking a clarifying question like 'So you're saying that...?'.

The aim is to assure the speaker that you are fully engaged and to ensure that you've accurately understood their point. This can dissolve preconceptions and open up new avenues of understanding. Chances are, she'll surprise you. And hey, if she doesn't, at least you've practiced the fine art of suspense.

Overcoming biases often involves the application of specific techniques, like Reflective Listening. Let me share an example to illustrate its transformative power. Take Judy, my friend from college who was always lively but seemed a bit down lately. I decided to check in with her, asking, "How have you been?".

With a shrug, she replied: "I'm alright, I guess."

Instead of moving on to another topic, I engaged in Reflective Listening.

"You guess? Sounds like there's more to it. What's going on?"

In that moment, her eyes widened, almost as if to say, "Thank you for really hearing me". She opened up about her recent struggles with work-life balance and how it was affecting her mental health. I continued to employ Reflective Listening, summarizing her concerns, and asking open-ended questions. By the end of our conversation, Judy said she felt lighter and more understood than she had in weeks. She also began to explore solutions to her problems, something she claimed she wouldn't have done without feeling truly heard. This simple act of Reflective Listening had sparked a shift in perspective, for both Judy and me.

Picture this: Bob, my poker-faced neighbor. We've been sharing a fence and occasionally forced smiles for years. Bob, a retiree, spends most of his day in his garage, tinkering away on some mysterious project. I always assumed our conversations would be as riveting as watching paint dry, so I never bothered to ask what he was working on. One day, whether led by curiosity or spurred by the power of Reflective Listening, I decided it was time for a real conversation.

I saw Bob, wrench in hand, and decided it was time to break the ice.

"Hey Bob, what's cooking in the innovation lab?" I asked.

Bob looked up, surprised, and then something extraordinary happened: he smiled and started sharing the details of a DIY solar panel he was working on. I listened, I mean *really* listened, and then used Reflective Listening to summarize what he said: "So you're essentially working on a green energy solution right in your own backyard. That's incredible!"

The glow on Bob's face could've powered his entire solar panel setup. Not only did I understand the depth of his passion, but Bob felt heard for the first time in what he said was a 'long while.' It was like we added a whole new color to the tapestry of our neighborly relationship, all thanks to Reflective Listening. My preconceptions? Shattered. Bob's enthusiasm? Ignited.

After mastering Reflective Listening, you'll find it easier to navigate complex conversational landscapes, even those typically dismissed as 'Echo Chambers', often used pejoratively to indicate a sealed-off room of similar perspectives. Yet, remember that time you were locked in a political debate with your uncle at a family dinner? You didn't parrot his views, but you listened, really listened. You echoed back his points before gently introducing your own. He felt heard, not bulldozed over, and suddenly, the term 'Echo Chamber' took on a different hue. It became a space where ideas were not just amplified but also dissected, reformed, and understood.

While adapting to different conversational styles is crucial, let's not overlook a universal aspect that fits in any scenario: the power of the pause. You know those moments of silence in conversations that most people awkwardly rush to fill?

They're not awkward; they're golden. Silence is the dramatic pause in a Shakespearean soliloquy, the pregnant pause before the punchline, the inhale and exhale of a mindful meditation.

It gives everyone a breather, a moment to marinate in the words and emotions that were just exchanged. So the next time you find yourself in one of these 'awkward' silences, don't just rush to fill it. Relish it. Let it be the space that allows the next note in your conversational melody to truly resonate.

Embracing the power of pause is crucial both offline and online. In this digital age, the platforms may change, but the essence of meaningful communication remains consistent. Except now, there's an orchestra of instruments: Emails are the stately violins, video calls the booming drums, and instant messages the nimble flutes. Each has its tune and rhythm. And let's not forget the ever-expressive emojis; they're the crescendos and diminuendos in our textual symphony. CAPS LOCK? Oh, that's our fortissimo, a deliberate stomp for emphasis. And that sneaky blue 'seen' tick? It's like the audience's nod, acknowledging the performance, but leaving you wondering if they actually enjoyed it or just endured it.

Think about the sensation of receiving a good, hearty hug. Now translate that into auditory form. It's when you're on the phone with a friend who's going through a hard time, and your voice and attention act as a comforting embrace. You can almost visualize the shoulders relaxing on the other end of the line. Unlike the awkward side-hugs of the pandemic era, auditory hugs know no distance or barriers. Your friend feels enveloped in care and warmth, even if you're miles apart.

Ever been at a comedy show where that one heckler in the audience thinks they're part of the act? Our inner critics can often be those annoying hecklers. Just last week, when your colleague was sharing their innovative idea in a meeting, that inner critic might have been too busy nitpicking the details to notice the brilliance of the broader concept. Learning to usher that inner heckler out of the auditorium of your mind, even just temporarily, can open up space for a genuinely enriching dialogue.

Now, you might be thinking, 'Why should I put in all this effort just to listen? I've got my own stuff to say'. Fair point. We all want to be the star of our own show. But consider this: If everyone's talking, who's actually listening? Plus, active listening isn't just for the person you're talking to; it benefits you too. It helps you get the whole picture, not just your slice of it. Kind of like putting on 3D glasses and seeing everything pop.

So, circling back to that opening question: 'How do I want them to feel at the end of the conversation?'

If you've managed to muzzle the multitasking monster, banish biases, adapt to the symphony of digital platforms, and respect the power of the pause, you've hit the conversational jackpot. Your friend, your neighbor, your colleague—they will walk away feeling heard, understood, and expanded in some indefinable yet palpable way.

In a world that often feels like a cacophony of voices clamoring for attention, the art of listening stands as a rare but transformative act. It's akin to holding up a sign that says, 'Your Voice Matters'. From pondering, 'How do I want them to feel at the end of the conversation?' to mastering the subtleties of active listening and the power of the pause, we've delved into what elevates a conversation from good to exceptional. Along the way, we've navigated the symphony of digital platforms, recognizing how they change the tone but not the essence of human connection. So let your conversations be the kind of echo that doesn't merely bounce back but resonates, amplifies, and creates a space for genuine interaction.

By now, you've been handed the proverbial toolbox filled with the instruments of empathetic and effective conversation: active listening, tackling biases, the 3-Second Rule, and even mastering the power of the pause. So what's next? The next conversation you have—whether it's with a loved one, a colleague, or even a stranger in a waiting room—apply just one of these tools. Make it your mission to make them feel heard, understood, and genuinely valued.

That's how you not only leave an indelible impression but also change the very dynamics of your relationships. In an age clamoring for the spotlight, remember: the most profound impact can come not from being the loudest in the room but from being the most attentive. Don't wait for the 'right moment' to be a better listener.

That moment is now.

Chapter Seventeen

Beyond Reciprocity

Are You a Person Others Want to Help?

"We cannot solve our problems alone; we need the help and wisdom of others."

— AUTHOR AND DESIGNER KAREN SALMANSOHN

So, here we all are, spinning on this planetary blue ball, often ending up in a bit of a pickle that requires a helping hand. Being human is a VIP pass to this help-seeking club, with no requirements for age, gender, or wealth. Maybe it's your friend offering a sympathetic ear during an emotional meltdown, or a random stranger offering a steadying hand in a crisis; our lives are stitched together with threads of assistance and kindness.

But here's the kicker: I'm not just referring to the act of giving or receiving help; I'm emphasizing the importance of becoming the kind of person whom others genuinely want to help.

True strength isn't a solo performance, but a group act, featuring a willingness to welcome the aid and wisdom of others while navigating the winding road of personal growth and success. This isn't just a neat idea—it's a profound truth applicable to all aspects of life. But to make space for the wisdom of others, one must first build a welcoming porch in the mind and heart.

Picture this: a boss, strong-willed and independent, has curated an image of herself as the alpha problem solver. But when faced with a challenge that demands external assistance, she freezes, afraid it may dent her self-crafted image. Thoughts like, 'Will asking for help strip me of my competency? Will it undermine my authority?' create a mental blockade against receiving help, signaling to her team that their input isn't valued.

The ripple effects are far from pleasant. A culture of collaboration fizzles out, creative idea exchange grinds to a halt, and a climate of uncertainty and fear replaces the once energetic and innovative environment. It's an unspoken decree: help-seeking equals weakness. The aftermath? A work culture in which people would rather suffer burnout than reach out for assistance.

So, how do you become someone people want to help? It starts with mental housekeeping. Challenge the self-reliance myths you've constructed and redefine what strength means. It doesn't mean being an island but, instead, having the courage to build bridges. Recognize that accepting help is an act of mutual respect and growth. If you accept help graciously and also acknowledge and appreciate it, you're sending an action-packed thank you note, showing people that their effort isn't lost on you.

The twist: being open to help also means being ready to pass on the baton of assistance and fostering a positive cycle of helpfulness. It doesn't necessarily mean repaying in kind or magnitude, but being ready to be the helper when someone else is in a tight spot. This creates a harmony of reciprocity, strengthening social ties and nurturing a sense of community.

Let's dive deeper for the keys in our cognitive and interpersonal dynamics. Our thoughts and interactions play a substantial role in our ability to give and receive help. It's all tucked into our social intelligence—the ability to navigate social mazes and understand social cues—which is crucial in nurturing a culture of assistance.

Cognitive psychology has an ace up its sleeve in this context and it's called theory of mind. This concept involves recognizing that people don't necessarily think and feel the same way we do. It grants us the ability to predict and interpret the actions of others. Think of it as being able to attune yourself to the perspectives of other individuals. This insight enables us to empathize, predict responses, and adjust our behavior accordingly. When we apply the theory of mind to seeking and offering help, it empowers us to truly understand the needs of others and respond with empathy, fostering an environment of openness and collaboration.

Let's say you've been assigned a tough task at work. You're struggling but fear of appearing incompetent stops you from asking for help. A perceptive colleague, using their theory of mind, might pick up on the struggle and offer to assist. Similarly, if in a position to help, understanding the hesitations of others will enable you to give support in a way that respects their autonomy, creating a safe space for collective problem-solving and learning.

Also, our biases and mental models, essentially our preconceived ideas of the world, can influence our help-seeking and help-giving behavior. For instance, the just-world hypothesis is a cognitive bias causing people to believe the world is fair and leading them to blame victims for their misfortune. This bias can result in reluctance to seek or provide help. Being aware of such biases can help us address them and foster a more supportive and inclusive environment.

As well, emotional intelligence, the ability to identify, understand, and manage emotions both within ourselves and in others is key. Emotionally intelligent people are better at building rapport, empathy, and mutual understanding, which are crucial in establishing a helpful relationship. An emotionally intelligent approach might involve being present, listening, and validating the feelings of another person. This approach respects their emotional state and autonomy, fostering a deeper connection and making it more likely they'll be open to receiving help.

Consider, for example, a friend who is going through a tough time. Rather than offering unsolicited advice (which can seem dismissive), an emotionally intelligent response might be to simply be present, listen, and validate their feelings. This approach creates an environment where they feel comfortable seeking help.

Our cognitive and emotional engagement with others plays a crucial role in fostering a culture of assistance. By honing our theory of mind, challenging our biases, and cultivating emotional intelligence, we can become individuals who not only offer help when needed but also create an environment where others feel safe and comfortable seeking help. This, in turn, enriches our own relationships, strengthens our communities, and enhances our shared human experience.

In the end, being open to help is about more than just receiving. It's about giving, sharing, and forging connections. It's about recognizing our shared humanity and our collective need for support. It's an invitation to others to be part of our lives, to contribute to our growth, and to strengthen the bonds that hold us together.

What behaviors and attitudes might influence others' perceptions of us? Are we individuals that others are willing to lend a helping hand to? Are we, in our interactions and behaviors, fostering a sense of community and supportiveness?

To truly understand and imbibe the ideas we've discussed, it's important to engage in some self-reflection. This set of reflective questions is designed to help assess our current approach and determine ways to become a person others want to help.

- Reflect on personal characteristics. What traits do you believe make someone the type of person whom others are willing to help? How do you embody these traits in your interactions?

- Have there been times when you refrained from asking for help due to fear of seeming less competent or undermining your authority? How might these fears be affecting others' willingness to help you?

- Might reluctance to seek help contribute to a stressful environment or a culture of burnout at the workplace or in personal relationships? What changes can you make to your approach?

- Reflect on your beliefs about self-reliance and strength. How might these be hindering others' willingness to help you? How could you redefine these concepts to be more open to assistance?

- Think about your relationships. Are you fostering a sense of reciprocity? If not, how could you cultivate this in your interactions?

- When has the theory of mind (the ability to comprehend mental states like beliefs, intents, desires, and emotions) been misapplied, leading to misunderstandings, or missed opportunities for help? How can you improve your understanding of others' perspectives?

- What biases might prevent others from wanting to help? How can you actively address these biases to foster a more inclusive environment?

- How does your level of emotional intelligence affect how others perceive you and their willingness to help? What steps could you take to improve your emotional intelligence?

- Reflecting on your current behaviors, why might someone hesitate to help you? What specific changes can you make to be seen as someone others would want to help?

- What personal barriers might be preventing you from becoming someone others want to help? How can you embrace humility and show appreciation more effectively?

Reflecting on these questions and assessing our behaviors, attitudes, and fears honestly, can provide invaluable insights into our current interactions and highlight areas for improvement. Remember, it's never too late to change. Being open to assistance, both in giving and receiving, involves acknowledging our shared human experience and embracing the benefits of collective problem-solving.

By encouraging collaboration, showing appreciation, and being ready to extend a helping hand, we can cultivate an environment where everyone feels valued and supported. In doing so, we become individuals others are eager to help, fostering a more compassionate and interconnected world in the process. The journey towards this goal starts with self-reflection and culminates in action. So, let's begin this journey today, with the intention of building a stronger, more supportive community for tomorrow.

Chapter Eighteen

Risky Business

Beyond the Safety Net

"Taking a risk doesn't mean you'll always win, but it does mean you'll always learn something valuable."

— AUTHOR, ENTREPRENEUR, AND MARKETING EXPERT SETH GODIN

The quote above, from Seth Godin, serves as a potent wake-up call, igniting the fire within us to defy convention, shatter limitations, and embark on a journey of audacious growth and awe-inspiring transformation.

Life can be a thrilling, heart-pounding adventure, teetering on the edge of exhilarating triumphs and gut-wrenching failures. It demands that we break free from the suffocating safety net and wholeheartedly embrace the tantalizing unknown. When embarking on new adventures, I often ask, 'How would I feel if I encountered failure, and could I handle the potential negative outcomes or consequences? How would I feel if I never took the chance and missed out on potential success?'.

In a world that values stability and security, taking risks becomes an act of rebellion. The siren song of certainty taunts us, vying to keep us confined within its suffocating embrace, shielding us from the vast mysteries and untapped potential that await us. But what do we gain by clinging to safety so tightly? Are we truly living, or merely existing?

Seth Godin challenges conventional notions fearlessly, emboldening us to step into discomfort, where true magic happens. Within the realm of these adventurous risks, we uncover priceless lessons and unearth unforeseen treasures, intricately shaping the very fabric of our existence. And in embracing risk, it is crucial to strike a delicate balance, avoiding the pitfalls of rash decisions. While we are urged to step into the unknown and challenge ourselves, it is essential to approach risks with thoughtful consideration and calculated strategies. The audacity to take risks must be accompanied by a discerning mindset that evaluates potential outcomes, weighs the costs and benefits, and aligns our actions with our core values and long-term aspirations. By combining daring courage with wise discernment, we can navigate the thrilling realms of risk-taking while minimizing impulsive choices that may derail us.

As we delve deeper into this realm, let's consider the following questions to gain a deeper understanding of the risks involved:

- What incredible treasures or game-changing breakthroughs might be possible if I dare to embrace this risk?

This question encourages exploration of potential positive outcomes such as personal growth, self-fulfillment, new horizons, and the chance to rise above the mundane. It provokes contemplation of how risk can contribute to our personal evolution, align with our ambitions, and ignite our sense of purpose and well-being.

- Are there lurking dangers or formidable consequences ready to test my mettle, and do I possess the courage to face them head-on?

This question compels us to scrutinize the potential hazards, pitfalls, and damaging aftermaths entangled with the risk. It forces us to ponder the ramifications for our relationships, finances, health, and overall well-being. We must also evaluate our resilience and readiness to accept and navigate these treacherous waters, weighing whether the rewards are worth the steep toll they might exact.

- How much of the outcome remains uncertain, and what critical insights must I uncover to make an informed and courageous decision? This question assesses the level of uncertainty surrounding the outcome. It compels us to consider the available intelligence, identify gaps in wisdom, and determine the sacred lore, research, or expertise required to make a calculated choice.

- Does this risk align seamlessly with my core beliefs and burning desire to make a significant impact in the world?

This question plunges us into introspection, calling us to reflect on whether the risk resonates with our deepest values, innermost yearnings, and the grand tapestry we envision for our future. It challenges us to explore how risk nourishes our personal evolution, aligns with our values, and fuels our pursuit of lofty goals.

- Do I have the audacity and resourcefulness to conquer the potential fallout of this endeavor?

This question requires an evaluation of our mettle and the resources we possess to navigate the treacherous path of risk, as we consider our emotional fortitude, financial stability, support networks, skills, and knowledge. Through this reflection, we can gauge whether we have the necessary tools or if we need to forge them.

- How have I defied the odds historically and bounced back from setbacks, and am I ready to fearlessly tackle this uncharted territory?

This question sheds light on our resilience and tenacity in the face of adversity. It compels us to reflect on how we have historically confronted challenges, setbacks, or failures in our lives. We must assess our ability to learn, adapt and persist amidst thorny obstacles. Through this introspection, we can determine our mental and emotional preparedness to confront potential setbacks or defeats associated with the risk.

- What whispers of intuition and unconventional wisdom beckon me to explore this risk, and what deep-seated fears or doubts must I confront along the way?

This question implores us to embrace the dark shadows within and trust the primal instincts that guide us through the storm. We must listen to the whispers of our gut, attuned to the underlying fears, doubts, or reservations that reverberate within us. Then, we must discern if they arise from rational considerations or if they are manifestations of anxiety or self-doubt.

By summoning these reflective questions, we gain clarity about our motivations, values, aspirations, and our tolerance for the potential risks. This heightened understanding empowers us to make informed decisions and navigate the treacherous jungle of risks with unwavering confidence and an unyielding sense of purpose.

In the face of daunting uncertainty, it is by embracing risk that we truly come alive. Risky business lures us to step beyond the comforting confines of the safety net and into the uncharted chasm of growth, fulfillment, and profound self-revelation. It challenges us to redefine our relationship with risk and to embrace its transformative power.

Let's consider the story of Mark, a seasoned executive working in a prominent corporation, who found himself at a crossroads that demanded a daring choice. Mark contemplated the risk of leaving his comfortable, well-established position to start his own consulting firm. As he grappled with the decision, he asked himself, 'What potential benefits or rewards can I gain by taking this risk?'.

Mark envisioned a life where he could use his expertise and insights to make a direct impact on organizations, drive meaningful change, and have the freedom to work on projects aligned with his passion. The potential positive outcomes of personal growth, professional fulfillment, and the ability to shape his own destiny resonated deeply within him. With this clarity, Mark summoned the courage to bid farewell to the corporate world and embark on the risky journey of entrepreneurship.

Despite the uncertainties that awaited him, Mark discovered newfound exhilaration, honed his consulting skills, and built a reputable brand which became known for delivering transformative results. Through taking the risk, Mark found himself on a path of self-discovery, where he forged his own way, built a network of clients and collaborators, and created a legacy based on his unique vision and expertise.

This story illustrates the power of calculated risk-taking in a business or organizational context, where individuals confront the daunting choice of leaving the safety and stability of a corporate career to pursue their entrepreneurial ambitions. It showcases the potential rewards of personal and professional growth, fulfillment, and the ability to leave a lasting impact in the business world.

Let's also consider the tale of John, a young and ambitious professional who found himself captivated by Mark's entrepreneurial journey. As he witnessed the transformative impact that Mark's consulting firm had made on several organizations, John felt a fire ignite within him and an insatiable desire to create his own business empire. He pondered the potential risks and negative consequences involved, asking himself, 'What are the potential risks or negative consequences, and am I willing to accept them?'.

John recognized that venturing into the realm of entrepreneurship would demand relentless dedication, unwavering commitment, and a willingness to navigate uncharted territories. However, he also acknowledged the potential rewards that awaited him: a chance to make a significant impact, build a legacy, and shape the industry with his visionary ideas.

With Mark's success story as inspiration, John summoned the courage to bid farewell to the corporate confines and embark on his own risk-laden journey.

Armed with meticulous planning and a deep understanding of his industry, John launched his own startup. He encountered countless obstacles and faced the harsh realities of entrepreneurship, but his unyielding spirit, strategic mindset, and relentless pursuit of excellence propelled him forward.

Through embracing the risk, John found himself on a transformative odyssey of self-discovery, crafting a successful business that surpassed his wildest dreams. His venture not only yielded financial rewards but also allowed him to leave an indelible mark on his industry, revolutionizing the way business was conducted.

Perched on the edge of uncertainty, we draw inspiration from others' narratives, summoning the courage to face our inner demons. We challenge ourselves to probe fearlessly, harnessing the transformative might of calculated risks. Deep within our introspection and bold pursuits we can find the keys to unlock a life lived to its fullest potential—one that escapes mediocrity, while embracing the extraordinary.

Through our journey into the realm of calculated risks, we unearth their transformative force. Inspired by tales of courage and self-reflection, we recognize that embracing risk sparks personal evolution and sets the stage for an enduring legacy. We meet uncertainties with unwavering resolve, fearlessly posing critical questions to shape our progress. Together, we chart a course through the stormy seas of risk and self-discovery, making a lasting impression.

As our journey ends, we carry forward the wisdom gained, setting sail on daring ventures, and crafting legacies that shatter mediocrity. By embracing risk, we ignite life and etch an unforgettable mark upon the world.

Chapter Nineteen

The Mind Maze

Clearing the Clutter for Clarity

"The biggest obstacle to clarity is believing we already have it."

— AUTHOR JULIA GALEF

Clarity often seems to be an elusive creature in the maze of our minds. As we pursue it, we weave through the knot of thoughts, emotions, and distractions, seemingly made by an overly enthusiastic kitten. Yet the allure of mental clarity draws us in, only to reveal that confusion is often self-inflicted.

Author Julia Galef aptly points out that one of the most significant obstacles to achieving clarity is the belief that we already possess it. To navigate this mental labyrinth, we must ask ourselves introspectively, 'What is muddling my thoughts and diverting my focus?'.

Our minds function like warehouses—stowing worries, fears, doubts, and desires. Each of these elements alone may be manageable, but their accumulation forms a dense fog, slowing down our thinking like outdated software. The interaction between these stored elements can be likened to a cacophony of voices talking all at once, each demanding your attention and pulling your focus in a different direction.

For instance, fears and doubts often reinforce each other, amplifying their intensity and making it difficult for rational thoughts and desires to pierce through. Meanwhile, distractions from the external world—like social media notifications or work emails—add an extra layer of noise, further diminishing your ability to focus.

The result? A mind cluttered not just by individual elements but by their complex interactions, making it a challenge to discern what truly matters. It's like navigating a storm where winds, rains, and waves synergistically create conditions far more perilous than any of these factors alone could produce. By shining a light on this chaos through introspection, we can begin to declutter not just the individual elements but also their tangled interactions.

Let's consider a few real-life scenarios where mental clarity is particularly crucial before we move on to specific, actionable steps to help clear your mental clutter.

First, we have the 'dilemma of the dream chaser'. Imagine an aspiring entrepreneur; a powerhouse fueled by passion and ambition. Suddenly, they find themselves sunk in the quicksand of entrepreneurship. Amidst this chaos, they hit pause and question, 'What's clouding my thoughts and muddying my focus?'.

This moment of self-contemplation reveals hidden fears and insecurities, stripping away cognitive layers to pave the way for a crystal-clear vision and a laser-focused path to success. Watch out, world!

Next is the emotional thrill ride, an exhilarating journey through the heart's depths. Picture someone caught in a storm of emotions, tossed around by waves of doubt and uncertainty. With a brave leap, they dare to ask, 'What's holding me back emotionally?'.

This courageous inquiry propels them into a deep exploration, uncovering emotional wounds, anxieties, and societal pressures that contribute to the chaos. Equipped with this newfound awareness, they can nurture relationships and find the strength to navigate towards a more peaceful emotional terrain.

Then we have the crossroads of the knowledge seeker. Picture a student at an academic fork in the road, burdened by societal expectations and plagued by self-doubt. Suddenly, a bold question arises: 'What's throwing me off and blurring my focus?'.

This question sparks deep soul-searching, where they discover their true passions and aspirations, freeing themselves from societal pressure. With this newfound self-awareness, they embark on an educational journey that's truly authentic and fulfilling. Who needs a GPS when lucidity shows the way?

Last, we have the personal odyssey. Imagine someone on a quest for personal growth, battling inner adversaries like negative self-talk and the fear of failure. Summoning bravery, they ask themselves, 'What's holding me back from achieving my personal growth?'.

This audacious inquiry unlocks the mental fortress, revealing self-imposed barriers and paving the way for significant growth and transformation.

In the pursuit of clear thinking, we must embrace a deeper understanding of this state itself. Mental clarity isn't just a destination but a state of being that empowers us to navigate life's complexities with purpose and confidence.

Now let's delve into practical steps that can aid us in our pursuit of cognitive clarity. These steps serve as a guide through the maze of our thoughts and emotions, offering a framework for unraveling the mental clutter and finding our way to a clearer and more purposeful mindset.

1. **Embrace the Beast:** acknowledge the challenge at hand; by recognizing and admitting the existence of mental clutter, we take the first, crucial step towards

a clearer, more organized mind.

2. **Unleash the Inner Inquisitor:** ignite introspection by asking hard-hitting questions; deep and sometimes uncomfortable inquiries into our thoughts and feelings can reveal insights that help dissolve confusion and establish clarity.

3. **Dive into the Abyss:** allow space for self-reflection, exploring emotions, fears, and limitations; by courageously delving into our innermost thoughts and fears, we create room for understanding and personal growth, a fundamental prerequisite for mental clarity.

4. **Expose the Culprits:** identify the root causes of confusion; by pinpointing the specific issues causing mental turmoil, such as unresolved emotions or unmet needs, we can address them directly and efficiently.

5. **Craft a Battle Plan:** develop a strategic blueprint for overcoming these challenges; creating a structured, practical plan helps dismantle mental clutter, providing concrete steps to navigate towards mental clarity.

6. **Embrace Grit and Grace:** recognize that mental clarity and personal growth require patience and persistence; achieving and maintaining mental

clarity is a continual process that demands
resilience, coupled with self-compassion when
progress seems slow, or stumbles occur.

7. **Perform Frequent Reality Checks:** regularly
   evaluate mental state, emotions, and progress; by
   continually checking in with ourselves, we can
   track our progress, adjust strategies as needed, and
   maintain our trajectory towards an uncluttered and
   clear mind.

A focused mind arises when the fog of confusion dissipates,
and we gain profound insight into our thoughts, emotions,
and aspirations. It involves more than just having a
transparent mind in a specific moment; it encompasses a
broader sense of self-awareness and understanding.

Clear thinking involves peeling back the layers of cognitive
clutter, unraveling the knots of doubt and uncertainty, and
delving into the depths of our inner landscape.

A clear mindset has transformative effects on multiple
aspects of our lives. One significant impact is on
decision-making. With unclouded minds, we can sift through
the noise of conflicting thoughts and emotions, enabling us
to make choices that align with our values and aspirations.
A focused mind helps us see the bigger picture, evaluate
options objectively, and assess potential outcomes with
sharper focus.

Moreover, clear thinking enhances problem-solving skills. It allows us to approach challenges with a calm and composed mindset, free from the fog of confusion and doubt. With a transparent thought process, we can analyze problems from various angles, identify root causes, and explore innovative solutions.

Mental clarity opens the door to creativity, enabling us to think outside the box and find novel approaches to overcome obstacles.

A transparent mind also plays a vital role in our relationships. When our minds are cluttered, it can be challenging to truly connect with others and understand their perspectives. However, when we cultivate clear thinking, we develop a heightened sense of empathy and emotional intelligence. This fosters deeper connections, effective communication, and more fulfilling relationships.

In addition to its impact on decision-making, problem-solving, and relationships, mental focus contributes to overall well-being. It brings a sense of calm and inner peace, allowing us to navigate life's challenges with grace and resilience. A clear mindset enables us to manage stress more effectively, promoting a healthier mental and emotional state.

Maintaining a clear mind involves adopting a holistic approach. Prioritize a healthy lifestyle through regular exercise, a balanced diet, and sufficient sleep. Cultivate mindfulness and stress management techniques. Limit screen time for a digital detox and engage in brain-stimulating activities such as reading, puzzles, and learning. Practice clear communication, maintain social connections, and limit multitasking. Take regular breaks, both outdoors and indoors, and consider seeking professional help if needed.

Cultivating a positive mindset is another essential strategy. Focusing on gratitude, optimism, and self-compassion allows us to navigate challenges with a clearer perspective. When we approach life with a positive outlook, we are better equipped to maintain mental focus, even in the face of adversity.

By incorporating these strategies into our daily lives and prioritizing them, we lay the foundation for ongoing clarity and personal growth. These practices become part of our lifestyle, helping us sustain a clear mindset and navigate life's twists and turns with greater ease and resilience.

Upon reflection, it becomes crystal clear that self-questioning is the ultimate weapon in dismantling mental barricades. Questions help us uncover the sneaky adversaries lurking in our subconscious, using the power of self-awareness as our beacon to navigate the labyrinth of our minds.

And remember to embark on this mind-boggling journey with a healthy dose of curiosity and compassion. Each thought and emotion, no matter how absurd or bewildering, has a story to tell. So, let's resist the urge to play judge and jury. Instead, let's embrace the vibrant spectrum of our experiences—both delightful and downright chaotic—as quirky travel companions on our quest for clarity.

Now, here's a little secret: our mental roadblocks often have their roots in societal conditioning and past experiences. Our minds, stubborn creatures that they are, cling to these beliefs like a security blanket, even when they're stifling our progress. But, armed with the superpower of consciousness, we can challenge those outdated notions and invite fresh insights into our lives. Time to evict those mental squatters and welcome the clarity that comes knocking.

What are the external temptations that try to lead us astray? The modern world, with its breakneck pace, and information overload—not to mention the alluring appeal of instant gratification—is like a mischievous siren song.

Navigating this maze of distractions requires mindfulness and intentional living. By choosing where to direct our mental energy, we regain control of our thoughts and chart a course towards clarity.

Decluttering our minds isn't a one-off cleanup session. It's a lifelong pact with self-discovery and evolution. Our minds require constant care and attention—much like a garden that needs regular pruning—and they crave our patience, perseverance, and a touch of tenacity. In return, our minds gift us the priceless treasure of an unwavering clarity to help us navigate life's twists and turns with conviction and grace.

With humility and an open mind, we can tap into the transformative power of self-awareness, uncover hidden gems, and move towards a clarity we all long for.

Chapter Twenty

Wantology

Uncovering Your True Desires

"Desire is the starting point of all achievement, not a hope, not a wish, but a keen pulsating desire which transcends everything."

— AUTHOR NAPOLEON HILL

Certainly, the resonance of Napoleon Hill's timeless insight can't be easily dismissed.

In a world addicted to immediate satisfaction, it's tempting to lounge on our sofas, snack mindlessly, and get lost in endless television episodes, all while nurturing a vague hope that our dreams will just happen. But Hill's words cut right through that illusion. He tells us it's not about hoping, or even wishing—desire is the catalyst for all achievement.

We might think we want success, love, and happiness served to us on a silver platter, maybe even with a side of fries. But the reality is far more demanding. If we truly want to achieve the kind of life-altering fulfillment that transcends the ordinary, we need to ignite a "keen pulsating desire" within us. That means rolling up our sleeves, stepping beyond the familiar, and taking the audacious, extraordinary actions that turn desires into reality.

Imagine this: we're craving that promotion at work, but all we do is show up, punch the clock, and scroll through cat videos. Well, guess what? That corner office isn't going to materialize out of thin air. We need to hustle, take risks, and unleash our very best inner badass. It's time to shake things up.

Wantology turns the whispers of your desires into a battle cry for action. It is not a mere wish list penned down on a whim; it's a refined list of innermost cravings, distilled from the murky waters of confusion and contradiction. This quasi-science, semi-art form acts as a decoder ring for adult life, translating the vague 'umms' and hesitant 'maybes' into a crisp syllabus of genuine desires. In an era awash with endless choices yet starved for true significance, mastering the art of Wantology is not just wanting what you have, but knowing what you want, offering a compass for your journey through the complex landscape of longing.

Wantology, with its thrilling and nerve-wracking escapades, encourages individuals to embrace uncertainty, challenge themselves, and embark on journeys of self-discovery that can lead to profound personal growth.

Wantology isn't just about the big dreams. It's about the little things too. It's about having the courage to try new hobbies, experiment with strange foods, and explore hidden passions. It's about infusing our life with a touch of curiosity and adventure. It's signing up for a pottery class, trying a spicy Thai dish, or learning to play the ukulele. We never know where these little acts of daring will lead us.

Let's take a look at how it manifests in real life, starting with Jake, a man who needed to overcome his fears to find his true self. Jake conquered his fear of public speaking through joining an improv group. It not only allowed him to challenge himself but also pushed him into uncharted territories of personal growth. 'Wantology', in Jake's case, involved embracing the unknown, taking risks, and immersing himself in an unfamiliar environment. As he took that freefall, the mischievous grin on his face symbolized the thrill and anticipation he felt.

In the beginning, Jake's venture into improv was nerve-wracking, but his determination to overcome his fear propelled him forward. Each session brought new challenges, forcing him to think on his feet and respond spontaneously, dancing on the edge of daring, teetering between success and failure. However, Jake persisted, and gradually, he began to discover a hidden talent for wit and quick thinking. His mischievous grin transformed into a genuine smile as he found himself commanding the stage with confidence.

Wantology allowed Jake to break free from the constraints of his introverted nature, unlocking a talent he never knew he had. By embracing the unknown with a wink and a nod, he not only conquered his fear but also rewrote his perception of himself.

Jake's journey exemplified the transformative power of Wantology, as he went from stuttering through sentences to becoming a captivating performer. His story serves as a testament to the profound impact that stepping out of one's comfort zone can have on personal growth and self-discovery.

Jake's journey through Wantology focused on conquering inner fears. But what happens when Wantology takes you out into the world? Enter Sarah, who redefined her life through exploration. Sarah broke free from her monotonous routine through a solo backpacking trip. Wantology, for Sarah, meant taking a leap of faith, leaving behind the familiar, and embracing the uncharted realms of adventure and exploration. The radiant smile on her face reflected the thrill she experienced while venturing into the unknown.

Sarah's decision to embark on a solo backpacking trip represented her desire to escape the monotony of her daily life and discover something more meaningful. She traded her comfortable office job for a journey that would redefine her perspective. With each step, she encountered new cultures, languages, and landscapes, challenging herself to adapt and navigate unfamiliar territories.

The freefall of Wantology pushed Sarah beyond her comfort zone, introducing her to jaw-dropping moments and mind-altering revelations. As she immersed herself in the rich tapestry of Southeast Asia, she discovered a sense of freedom she had never experienced before.

Through Wantology, Sarah uncovered her true desires and rewrote the story of her life. The journey awakened her sense of adventure, leading to new experiences and a more fulfilling lifestyle. Sarah's story exemplifies how Wantology can empower individuals to break free from societal expectations, rediscover their passions, and create a life that aligns with their authentic selves.

In both Jake and Sarah's stories, Wantology enabled them to embrace the unknown, push their boundaries, and ultimately transform their lives. By moving into uncharted realms, they unlocked hidden talents, rewrote their stories, and discovered a newfound sense of purpose and fulfillment.

While Sarah found herself in far-off lands, Wantology isn't always about grand journeys. Sometimes it's about finding joy in life's smaller moments, like Brenda discovered on the dance floor. Brenda was a middle-aged accountant who decided to take up salsa dancing. She stumbled her way through the steps, feeling self-conscious and out of her element.

But as she twirled and spun on the dance floor, something magical happened. Brenda found joy in movement, liberation in self-expression, and a newfound confidence that spilled into every aspect of her life. By embracing her desire for dance, Brenda transformed herself from a wallflower into a vibrant force of energy.

Now, I won't sugarcoat it. Wantology isn't a smooth ride. We'll stumble, we'll fall, and we'll probably end up with a few bumps and bruises. But that's part of the thrill, right? It's about pushing past our limits, defying expectations, and showing the world what we're truly made of.

Brenda's transformation was personal and liberating, but Wantology can also fuel professional aspirations. Sam's tale is one of entrepreneurial resilience and determination. Sam was a young entrepreneur with a string of failed business ventures. He faced rejection, financial setbacks, and the crushing weight of self-doubt. But instead of giving up, Sam dug deep and decided to launch a brand-new venture, completely out of his comfort zone.

This time, armed with hard-earned wisdom and an unyielding determination, he defied the odds and built a successful business empire. By doing something he had never done before, Sam not only achieved his dreams but also learned the invaluable lesson that failures are simply steppingstones to success. Sam's tenacity showcases Wantology's role in achieving professional dreams.

Inspired? Let's discuss some actionable steps that will help you jump-start your own journey through Wantology.

1. **Break the Couch Potato Cycle:** It's time for us to rise from the ashes of mediocrity; to put down the chips and turn off the TV, and step into the arena of possibility. Success, love, and happiness won't appear like a genie out of a bottle. We must unleash our inner adventurers, push our boundaries, and embark on a voyage of astonishing discoveries.

2. **Embrace the Uncomfortable:** If we want to taste fulfillment, we must be willing to embrace the discomfort. It's time to hustle, take risks, channel our inner maverick, and shake things up like a hurricane, defying expectations and showing the world what we're truly made of.

3. **Dive into Wantology:** Picture bungee jumping into the unknown, wearing a flaming tutu, with a pack of wild monkeys cheering us on. I know. It's almost impossible to imagine. But instead of fighting that image, embrace the thrilling, exhilarating, and yes, even scary aspects of Wantology. It's in the daring leaps that magic happens.

4. **Small Acts of Daring:** Wantology isn't just about

the big dreams; it's about sprinkling our lives with a dash of curiosity and adventure. An unexplored art exhibit, the flavors of a fiery Mexican dish that sets our palate on fire, or the harmonious strings of a mandolin can steer us towards uncharted territories.

5. **Embody Jake's Courage:** Take inspiration from Jake, the self-proclaimed introvert who conquered his fear of public speaking. Joining an improv group, diving into a world of spontaneity and watching as our confidence blooms can transform our lives.

6. **Channel Sarah's Wanderlust:** Break free from the monotonous routine. Embarking on that solo backpacking trip, traveling, and exploring new territories that ignite our sense of adventure invites us to embrace different cultures and set our spirit free. Let's be guided by our longing for exploration to uncover our true desires.

7. **Unleash Brenda's Vibrance:** Just like Brenda's love of salsa dancing, it's time for us to embrace our hidden passions. Take up a dance class, stumbling through the steps, and let the rhythm awaken a vibrant force and find joy in movement, liberation in self-expression, and watch as it spills into every aspect of life.

8. **Embrace the Challenges:** Wantology isn't a smooth ride; expect stumbling blocks, falls, and a few

battle scars along the way. It's in those moments of challenge and resilience that we grow stronger. Embrace the thrill of pushing past limits and defying the odds. You are a force to be reckoned with.

9. **Embody Sam's Determination:** Take a page from Sam's book, the entrepreneur who faced failure but rose again. When faced with setbacks, we won't let them crush our spirit. We're going to dig deep, gather the lessons learned, and launch a brand-new venture outside our comfort zones and on the path to success.

Let's silence those doubting voices, embrace the audacity of our desires, and act as never before. All this to say, it's time to unleash our inner dream-chaser and silence those doubting voices in our head. Remember, life is too short for mediocrity and settling for the ordinary. Take a leap of faith, dance with the unknown, and watch as the universe conspires to make our wildest dreams come true. Because when we're willing to do what we've never done, we'll discover a world of endless possibilities, a world where our true desires can finally take flight.

Chapter Twenty-One

Pause, Ponder, and Flip the Script

The Power of Intentional Decision-Making

"Decision is a sharp knife that cuts clean and straight; indecision, a dull one that hacks and tears and leaves ragged edges behind it."

— RETIRED POLICE OFFICER GRAHAM GORDON

Graham Gordon's words above slice through the heart of our relationship with decision-making, capturing the essence of its impact.

Decision-making is a powerful tool, capable of either bringing clarity and progress or causing confusion and stagnation. The choice between a well-wielded blade and an unwieldy chopper ultimately rests with us. However, amidst the hustle and bustle of life, we often overlook the fact that decision-making itself is a decision, a choice we must make consciously.

Consider the world around us, a hyper-caffeinated, overzealous creature, moving constantly at breakneck speed, leaving us in its wake. Choices whiz by like items on a supercharged conveyor belt, and the mantra of 'hurry up' seems to echo everywhere we turn. It is easy to feel like a small cog in this turbocharged mechanism, effortlessly swept along by its momentum. But what if we were to pause for a moment, to step back and evaluate our options with intentionality?

Picture yourself standing at the crossroads of life; one path adorned with the alluring, low-hanging fruit of instant gratification, whispering enticing tales of an easy and comfortable existence. Yet, there is a deeper sense within you, a knowing that there is more to life than the path of least resistance. With a wry smile, you tap into the magic of intentional decision-making—a wink, a nod—and suddenly, you become the one setting the direction. With a sense of purpose, you tap into the realm of intentional decision-making, ready to embark on a journey of self-discovery and empowered choices.

This is the clandestine world of introspection, which transforms the ordinary into the extraordinary. Imagine it as your own grand ballroom, where thoughts, emotions, and choices vie for the lead in an intricate dance. But here, you are not an unthinking follower; instead, you are the maestro, orchestrating every dip, twirl, and step. A master choreographer, you consider every rhythm and movement, tapping into the depths of your innate rhythm to execute a dance sequence that is quintessentially 'you'.

Intentional decision-making is not a whimsical philosophical exercise; it is a golden invitation to a tomorrow that brims with possibilities and untapped potential. It pulses with the hidden power that resides within each of us. Here's the grand strategy:

Know ourselves: By pausing and pondering before making decisions, we transform into emotional detectives, deciphering the patterns and clues in our own behavior. Like seasoned sleuths, we piece together the fragments of our psyche. This self-knowledge equips us to navigate the intricate maze of our emotions, enabling us to make decisions that mirror our true selves.

For example, let's say you're considering a career change. Pause and ponder to understand what brings you true fulfillment and aligns with your values. Reflect on your past experiences, moments of joy and fulfillment, and identify the common threads that run through them. This self-awareness will guide you in making a decision that reflects your true self.

Cultivating self-discovery is akin to mastering the introspective samba. We turn the mirror inward and bravely confront the tough questions. What ignites our passion? What leaves us indifferent? How well do we understand our own behavior patterns and tendencies?

As we become more proficient in this dance, self-awareness becomes an automatic step in our routine, guiding us effortlessly through the decision-making process.

Play the long game: Who among us hasn't been the unsuspecting moth, lured by the transient and destructive flame of immediate gratification, only to be left singed and regretful? Intentional decision-making empowers us to resist this transient siren song, allowing us to glimpse the domino effect our choices can set in motion.

Imagine you have a tempting offer to start a business that promises quick financial gains. Pause and consider the potential long-term consequences. Explore the challenges, risks, and sustainability of the venture. By playing the long game, you can make an intentional decision that aligns with your long-term goals and values.

Like learning the tango, playing the long game requires balance and poise. The more we resist knee-jerk reactions and anticipate the long-term effects of our choices, the more harmoniously we dance in sync with our goals. We must ask, 'Have we fallen into the trap of immediate gratification in the past? How can we develop the ability to resist short-term temptations and focus on long-term consequences? What strategies can we employ to anticipate the ripple effects of our decisions?'.

Guts and gumption: Life's journey is rife with unexpected twists, challenges that trip us up, and moments that leave us breathless. However, through intentional decision-making, we can embrace the absurdities, transforming obstacles into opportunities for growth and self-expression. We become fearless players, turning challenges into a performance art.

Let's say you encounter a major setback in your personal life, such as a relationship ending or a career setback. Embrace the challenge with guts and gumption. Pause to reflect on your strengths and resilience and use intentional decision-making to bounce back stronger. Embrace the opportunity for personal growth and view the setback as a steppingstone to a more fulfilling future.

This dance is our resilience rumba, where every stumble becomes an opportunity to rise again with even greater fervor. Maintaining rhythm, regardless of life's changing beat, becomes the key. We must reflect on how we currently handle adversity or unexpected challenges. How can we cultivate resilience and bounce back stronger from setbacks? Are there any fears or doubts that hold us back from making intentional decisions, and how can we address them?

Connect and conquer: Intentional decision-making is not a solitary endeavor; it is about how our choices resonate with others and the impact our collective energy has on the world around us. By choosing to reflect before reacting, we become listeners who hear the unspoken, allies who comprehend, and friends who empathize.

Consider this: Your team is facing a difficult decision. Instead of rushing into a solution, take the time to listen actively to your teammates' perspectives, their concerns, and aspirations. By empathizing and connecting with your colleagues, you can decide what not only benefits you but also positively impacts the team and the overall environment.

This step is akin to a well-coordinated troupe of intentional decision-making. Mastering it requires cultivating empathy and active listening, attuning ourselves to the unspoken words and feelings of those around us. How well do we listen to others and truly understand their perspectives? How can we improve our ability to empathize with those around us? In what ways can our decisions positively impact the people and environment around us?

Let's hold up a mirror for the skeptics out there. Intentional decision-making is not an endless journey of self-absorption, nor is it a state of perpetual indecision. It is the sublime dance of thought and action. It's about knowing when to trust our collective instincts and take the leap, and when to retreat and view the panorama of our decisions from a broader perspective.

Our decisions shape us, much as a chisel shapes stone. Intentional decision-making is the precision tool that allows us to ascend to the helm of our fate, carving out our unique place in the world. The allure of intentional decision-making lies in recognizing that every decision we make etches into the marble block of our destiny.

The ultimate goal is not always to make the 'right' decisions. It is about reveling in the mystery of self-reflection, understanding our drives and motivations, weighing the long-term consequences carefully, forging sturdy and reciprocal relationships, and making decisions that resonate with our core selves. It is about decision-making with resolve, purpose, and a daring spirit of exploration. Now, that's a dance worth dancing.

Chapter Twenty-Two

Alchemy

From Intention to Result

"The universe doesn't give you what you ask for with your thoughts; it gives you what you demand with your actions."

— Behavioral Science Academic Steve Mariboli

Steve Mariboli's insights remind us that the path from dreaming to doing isn't powered by wishful thinking but by decisive action. The universe listens not to our silent wishes but to our active pursuits.

When we live with intention, we transcend mere existence in the physical realm and become pioneers in an untamed frontier of endless opportunity. In this limitless expanse, our intentions are no longer just thoughts but catalysts for action. They become the force that shapes our lives, influences our environments, and orchestrates the unique melody of our existence.

Intentions are not fleeting thoughts; they are powerful surges that ripple through the tangible universe, setting off waves of change, and synchronizing with cosmic forces. Each intention acts as a stone thrown into the calm waters of reality, making ripples that alter the course of our lives and shape our future with every expanding wave.

By embracing intentionality, we no longer ride the roller coaster of life passively. Instead, we seize control and tap into our inner potential. With awareness, we influence the contours of existence. We are no longer drifting through circumstances; we are taking charge, using our power to shape reality according to our will.

In this vast expanse of infinite possibility where our potential thrives, intentions become the tools that open the doors to our desired future. By standing firm in our intentions, we send a strong signal to the universe, expressing our deepest desires explicitly. The universe acts as our cosmic ally, aligning with these signals and weaving them into the intricate tapestry of our life's journey.

However, we must not overlook the essential relationship between intention and mindfulness. Mindfulness amplifies our intentions allowing them to take center stage in our awareness, enhancing their power, and broadcasting our desires boldly to the universe. Mindfulness solidifies our intentions, transforming them from fleeting whispers into a resounding declaration of our earnest ambitions.

As we navigate the exhilarating terrain of personal growth, we come to understand that intentions not only guide the direction but also lay the foundation. They bridge the gap between our current reality and the vibrant life we yearn for.

Intentions act as master builders. They construct towering skyscrapers of accomplishments and trace the intricate plotlines that narrate our life stories. By choosing empowering beliefs consciously and aligning them with dynamic intentions, we ignite a revolution within ourselves. We become reality hackers, turning our limitations into launching pads for boundless opportunities.

Throughout this rebellious journey, one truth becomes crystal clear: intentions are not mere seeds scattered in the wind; they are the Swiss army knife that pries open the gates to our dreams. They possess the power to reshape our reality, transforming the mundane into the extraordinary and the mediocre into the exceptional.

But why do intentions carry such weight? The answer lies in the intricate dance between our compass of intentions, the vibrant symphony of thoughts, the choreography of actions, and the steady rhythm of behaviors. When these elements harmonize, our reality unfolds like a captivating masterpiece, an exquisite painting that tantalizes the senses and captivates the soul.

However, let us not deceive ourselves into thinking that intentions alone can shape our reality.

Intentions without action are like an amplifier without electricity: powerless. It is when we combine our intentions with bold and purposeful action that our dreams materialize into tangible realities, inviting us to revel in their splendor.

And so, I present these unfiltered, impactful tips for setting intentions:

Dive Deep into Your Desire: Explore the unfathomable depths of your soul fearlessly, unveiling hidden treasures and unspoken longings. Within these depths lies the launchpad for intentions that hold weight and authenticity.

Self-Awareness: Your Personal GPS: Get to know your inner landscape like an expert cartographer mapping unexplored terrain. Navigate the contours of your emotions, patterns, and motivations. This personal GPS won't let you down—it's calibrated to lead you to intentions that are authentically 'you'.

Paint Your Intentions in HD: If your intentions are a blur, your results will be a smudge. So, ditch the low-res, vague intentions. Define them in vibrant HD. Go for crystal clear, sharp-as-a-tack specifics. This clarity turns your intentions from mirages into solid, touchable realities.

Feel the Heat, Fuel the Flame: Emotions are the secret sauce that add zing to your intentions. Taste the joy, feel the peace, and let the energy of your emotions supercharge your intentions. Turn up the heat and watch your intentions sizzle.

Be the Positivity Prodigy: When it comes to setting intentions, remember this simple mantra: 'Negativity is out; positivity is in'. Channel your inner positivity prodigy. Put out the vibes you want to receive and, like a cosmic boomerang, they'll come right back.

Action: The Secret Ingredient: A potent potion without the secret ingredient is like an intention without action: lackluster. So, stir in some action, let it simmer, and watch your intentions come alive. It's the perfect recipe.

Patience: The Art of Cosmic Cool: When it comes to manifestation, time's a trickster. It loves to test your patience. But here's the catch: stay cool. Cosmic cool. The universe is always on time, even when it *appears* to be late.

Intention Tune-Up: Our journey is an ever-changing road trip. Don't forget to pull over for regular 'intention pit stops'. Refuel, recalibrate, and—if necessary—reroute. Keep your intentions in line with the evolving GPS coordinates.

The Fiesta of Progress: Each stride toward an intention is a cause for celebration. So, throw a mini fiesta each time. These victories, no matter how small, are checkpoints on the route to a grand destination. Enjoy the journey, and remember, the path to progress is always under construction.

Intentions act as turbo boosters, propelling us from the ordinary to the extraordinary on the exhilarating ride of life. However, intentions alone cannot steer the course; it is up to us to grasp the wheel. So, buckle up your intentions firmly in the driver's seat. Engage the gears, navigate the twists and turns, and bear witness as reality transforms into a magnificent tapestry of your own creation.

Allow me to share three vivid illustrations of intention's transformative power:

First, imagine the dance of career success, where two individuals with similar qualifications compete for a coveted promotion. One approaches the opportunity with a burning intention and relentless determination to excel, while the other wanders aimlessly without a clear purpose.

The outcome is predictable. The one with unwavering intention, fueled by aligned action, secures the coveted prize. When intention harmonizes with action, it propels us towards achievement.

Now, take a stroll through the enchanting gardens of relationships. Picture a person nurturing the intention to cultivate deep, meaningful connections. Their intention acts as a magnet, attracting like-minded souls into their orbit. These connections flourish and lead to fulfilling relationships. Conversely, without a clear intention, relationships may remain shallow and unfulfilling.

Witness the alchemical action that occurs in the magic of life. By setting an intention to prioritize wellbeing and pair it with consistent effort, the transformations are awe-inspiring. However, without a clear intention, these spells are as effective as decaf coffee on a weary Monday morning, lacking the power to invigorate and uplift.

This principle extends its magnificence to personal growth, much like the metamorphosis of a caterpillar into a splendid butterfly. An intention to blossom personally, coupled with unwavering dedication, becomes the necessary cocooning phase. It paves the way for the inevitable breakthrough, as we spread our wings and soar into the realm of learning, growth, and boundless possibilities. Without such intention, we may remain a caterpillar forever, confined to the limitations of crawling on the ground, never realizing the expanse of the skies above.

These narratives illuminate the transformative power of intentions. With a clear artistic vision, you become the master artist, skillfully painting thoughts and actions onto the canvas of existence. Intentions guide the brush, shaping the strokes and colors that create the beautiful symphony of experiences. Refining this artistry and breathing life into our vision, can unlock the hidden potential of the creator.

Moreover, this alchemical magic extends far beyond personal transformation and into the realms of collective impact. Our individual intentions possess the power to ripple through the world around us, creating a tidal wave of positive change that transcends the boundaries of self. When intentions grounded in love, compassion, and abundance are collectively held, they become an unstoppable force for transformation.

The power of intentions is formidable; they are catalysts for growth, architects of our reality, and bridges that connect our desires with tangible results. By harnessing this alchemy, we unlock our transformative potential and stride confidently towards a life brimming with purpose, fulfillment, and extraordinary accomplishments.

At the crack of dawn (or before the chaos of the world descends), take a precious moment for introspection. Consider these five pivotal questions to set intentions for yourself and your role in this grand tapestry called life:

1. What is my intention for myself today? Which personal goals, desires, or qualities will I prioritize and embody throughout the day, propelling me towards growth and fulfillment?

2. What is my intention for my role as [insert role]? How can I bring my best self forward and make a positive impact in every interaction and responsibility, leaving a meaningful mark?

3. How can I infuse my relationships with compassion and kindness today? What intentions can I set to foster understanding, empathy, and unwavering support in my connections with others, strengthening the bonds we share?

4. What is my intention for my work or professional life? How can I make significant progress, achieve my

goals, and contribute to my organization or field in a purposeful and impactful way, working towards a lasting legacy?

5. What intentions can I set to prioritize self-care, maintain a healthy balance, and cultivate inner peace and fulfillment, nurturing my overall well-being and enabling me to thrive?

These powerful questions can act like a shot of caffeine for focus and attention, a compass that guides our decisions in conscious living. By shaping our day with intention and purpose, we have the power to make a profound impact not only on our own lives but also in the lives of those around us. Manifesting intentions requires unwavering discipline, dedication, and focus. Yet, the reward is a reality infused with boundless potential: the power to transform not only ourselves but the very world we inhabit.

Chapter Twenty-Three

The Paradoxical Mind

A Neurological Tango

"The test of a first-rate intelligence is the ability to hold two opposed ideas in the mind at the same time, and still retain the ability to function."

— AMERICAN NOVELIST F. SCOTT FITZGERALD

The paradox is as essential to human thought as oxygen is to life. Or is it? Already, we are in a paradox.

According to F. Scott Fitzgerald, the celebrated American novelist, wisdom is precisely the ability to juggle these mind-bending contradictions; to accept and contain them within our jam-packed minds, while maintaining a healthy credit score, showing up to work on time, and remembering our anniversary, captures the essential nature of paradoxes.

We acknowledge the contradictions. If we reject them, well, we fall straight into another contradiction.

It seems that the human mind, in its beautiful complexity, has an intrinsic affinity for paradoxes. Fitzgerald knew it, and your mail carrier may know it too. After all, they're always whistling cheerily while trudging through the rain, paradoxically seeming both miserable and delighted.

Consider the paradox of hedonism, which asserts that pleasure is the only thing worth pursuing; yet the more we pursue it, the more elusive it becomes.

Or consider the paradox of choice: the more options we have, the less satisfied we tend to feel with our decisions.

Paradoxes—those tricky beasts—have sneaked their way into the very fabric of existence; impish characters leaving a paradoxical breadcrumb trail that challenges our grip on reality.

Take a moment and consider the paradox of control and surrender. The cognitive virtuoso in us performs a delightful ballet around this conundrum. We know there are moments when we must clutch the reins, exert our will, and guide life in our preferred direction. Yet, simultaneously, we acknowledge the necessity of loosening our grip, letting the river of life carry us along in its current. This dance is the paradoxical mind's *pièce de résistance*—a testament to its elegant adaptability.

Often, we overlook the cosmic joke that life plays on us: our pursuit of order creates the very chaos we strive to eliminate. Here lies a tantalizing irony. Our inherent instinct drives us to solve puzzles and mend fractures in understanding, yearning for a simple and orderly universe. Yet, our quest for simplicity stirs up disorder.

We can become self-sabotaging cleaners, inadvertently creating more mess with each attempt to declutter. Thus, we find ourselves trapped in a cycle, fueled by our pursuit of clarity, which paradoxically weaves an even more complex web. The irony is both amusing and profound: our desire for resolution ignites the fire of confusion.

In this age of interconnectedness and digital acceleration, the ability to hold multiple perspectives in peaceful coexistence has become more crucial than ever. Our challenges, whether they manifest as technological gaps, social disparities, or environmental concerns, demand complex solutions.

They require us to break free from our rigid mental cubicles and immerse ourselves in the bustling open-concept office of human thought. As we have discovered, attempting to untangle life's intricate complexities often feels like troubleshooting an expansive and intricate system. Nonetheless, we are up to the task. After all, the journey towards resolution frequently involves unexpected detours through the web of paradox.

Leadership is another realm that's being shaken profoundly by the paradoxical mind. In an age in which simple solutions are about as useful to us as a bicycle is to a fish, good leaders must dance with the contradictions that characterize our era. They must deftly navigate the delicate balance between the urgency of short-term goals and long-term sustainability; between the comforting solidity of stability and the exhilarating fluidity of adaptability; between the structure of hierarchy and the freedom of empowerment. These are the leaders who can maintain a delicate equilibrium between opposing forces, drawing from their wisdom to guide their teams through the tumultuous sea of the modern world.

But why do we persist in such a paradox-ridden existence? Perhaps contradictions are the mind's way of ensuring that it always has something on which to work. The treadmill of thought and the endless loop of reflection keeps our intellectual muscles flexed. Moreover, these cognitive conundrums can lead us to critical insights and breakthroughs.

The eureka moments that redefine our understanding of the world often emerge from a hearty wrestling match with paradoxes. We recall that the Earth is both incredibly vast and infinitesimally small when considered in the universe's grand context. These contradictions may appear frustrating at first, but they often prove fertile ground for new concepts, theories, and innovations.

One might say, 'Alright, but how does this affect me? I'm no philosopher, nor a neuroscientist. Why should I care?'.

A fair point.

We care because we live our lives steeped in contradictions. We are mortal beings who dream of immortality; creatures of habit who crave novelty; beings who, in seeking independence, can't escape the interconnected web of existence. Every day we're tasked with navigating these paradoxes and somehow—against all odds—we manage. It's a wonder and testament to human adaptability, ingenuity, and resilience.

To illustrate how these paradoxes play out in our daily professional lives, allow me to share a personal experience that put my own paradoxical thinking to the test.

One day, I received a phone call from my cousin, which presented a peculiar dilemma. She found herself caught between conflicting emotions: anger and affection. The source of this paradox was her son, who had covered his bedroom walls in a whirlwind of permanent marker.

This act of juvenile creativity was cause for discipline, and her initial impulse to punish him. However, the twist came when she discovered the scrawled message, 'I love you, Mommy'. That sentiment elicited a strong wave of love, hence her contradictory impulse to hug him. A minor incident, perhaps, but a perfect manifestation of the paradoxes we navigate daily.

But that's the delight, isn't it? Embracing the contradictions, the unresolvable, the paradoxical nature of existence is not just a mark of wisdom; it is the art of living. In recognizing the simultaneous truths of the absurd and the profound, the joyous and the tragic, the mundane and the miraculous, we are led to an even greater understanding of what it means to be human.

To illustrate the curious power of this paradoxical mind, let me recount an experience. One afternoon, an intriguing email landed in my inbox. It bore a request from an Australian coaching psychologist in search of a keynote speaker for their conference, set to take place six months down the road. The reference for my name came from a colleague at the prestigious Harvard Institute of Coaching, and this recommendation was seconded by a former client of mine, an American expatriate residing in Australia.

The request intrigued me. They had never encountered anyone open to discussing work within a traumatic context, let alone someone operating as a Shadow Coach. It piqued their interest further as many of my clients at the time were involved in intense fields such as plane crash investigations, managing disasters like tsunamis and earthquakes, operating in war zones, and serving on specialized task forces, including firefighters and security specialists. This suggested that I could illustrate a methodology that was entirely new to them in a context they weren't familiar with.

I was really excited about this possibility, so saying no wasn't an option, despite it squeezing its way between two other engagements—an Emergent Leaders program I was conducting in Chicago and a TED event where I was speaking. It meant flying across the globe, cramming in six precious days. Yet, without a moment's hesitation, I seized the chance and accepted the invitation enthusiastically.

The gears in my mind immediately started turning, mapping out the contours of my speech and envisioning the accompanying slides. To demonstrate the curious power of this paradoxical mind, let me share something that unfolded over a series of weeks. I consulted with the Australian coaching psychologist who extended the invitation, over a Zoom call.

As we chatted, he confessed: "You're insane to do this work, and I have the clinical credentials to back it up!"

We laughed, but his words carried a genuine undercurrent of admiration. I took it as a compliment.

However, the universe seemed to have a wicked sense of humor. Just an hour later, another email popped into my inbox, pressing me to hold a pre-conference workshop on Shadow Coaching® the day before the main event. Naturally,

I couldn't resist this additional opportunity to share my work and promptly agreed.

But alas, the cosmic mischief wasn't yet satisfied. After another hour elapsed, an email arrived from my former client, proposing a joint panel discussion with my Harvard colleague. Suddenly, I found myself burdened with the task of preparing not one, not two, but three distinct modules for this conference.

As if this juggling act weren't enough, the phone began to ring incessantly. First, it was my Harvard colleague on the line, cautioning me to frame my talk in a way that wouldn't rattle the attendees. They implored me to emphasize that my coaching psychology model wasn't a one-size-fits-all solution. Next came the call from my American client temporarily working in Australia, who echoed a similar sentiment: "Please, don't unleash the full force of your Donna way of working upon them."

These calls brought me to an abrupt stop. The paradox struck me forcefully, leaving a tinge of irony: these admirable people had praised my work for its boldness, yet now their conversations implied, 'Tone it down!'. Caught in this conundrum, a strategic chess match played out in my mind: should I listen to these experienced colleagues or follow my own instincts?

I knew what I had to do. Well-intentioned as they might have been, the ultimate decision rested with me. And so, I embarked on the journey to Australia.

The initial workshop, a mere teaser, sought to provide a glimpse into my groundbreaking methodology. I set the tone with the story of my two respected colleagues and their divergent advice. I challenged the group by saying: "You can sit there, listening to what I have to say, and scoff, 'This woman is utterly wacko!' or you can open your mind and consider the possibilities."

By the time the first break arrived, a queue had formed. People awaited their turn to engage in conversation eagerly, urging me to return the following year. The organizers had already charted a nationwide lecture tour for my return.

Within this narrative resides a profound lesson about the intricate workings of the human mind. It unveils our ability to confront opposing guidance, perceive the subtle interplay of paradoxes, and above all, make autonomous choices that uphold our proficiency and principles. As we embrace the tensions and intricacies inherent in every situation, we unveil fresh horizons, sparking both personal and professional advancement.

The next time you stand at a crossroads, besieged by conflicting advice, find solace in this tale. Always recall, the contradiction within your thoughts is not a bug—it's a feature. In the words of an age-old adage, 'The only way out is through'. Yet, paradoxically, do we *truly* wish to emerge on the other side?

Part Three: Radical Acceptance

Embodying Authenticity, Mindfulness, and Self-Acceptance

"Fitting in and belonging are two separate things. Fitting in involves people changing themselves in order to be accepted. Belonging allows people to be accepted as they are."

— RESEARCHER, AUTHOR, AND SPEAKER BRENÉ BROWN

The quote above from Brené Brown highlights the concept of radical self-acceptance as a powerful response to a culture that perpetually undermines our sense of worth.

Let's focus on obliterating the hurtful notion that we are, in any way, 'not enough'. The time has come to embark on our unique journey toward radical acceptance, with great gusto and undeterred joy.

Gear up as we unveil the spellbinding trifecta that'll set us free: authenticity, mindfulness, and self-acceptance. Authenticity is our first step—the undaunted antidote to the incessant pressures of a meticulously curated world. We shall parade our genuine selves, unadorned and unapologetic, brushing shoulders with vulnerability and basking in the rebellious glow of imperfections.

Mindfulness steps in as the central pillar of our awe-inspiring movement, transforming our inner rebel into an empathic, present ally. It's an art that teaches us to live in the present, tossing aside the shackles of past failures and fears of the future. We're redecorating our mental space with peace, tranquility, and a hefty dash of self-love. Mindfulness provides the unwavering roadmap to our journey.

At the summit of this uprising lies the crown jewel: self-acceptance. We'll fully embrace every beautiful and messy part of our lives, facing our fears and challenges head-on, and finding a healthier, happier self along the way. We'll dance through the storms, refashioning our faults and fears into whimsical streamers, and throw caution—and pretense—to the wind.

This is our time to move toward mindfulness, authenticity, and self-acceptance so ruthlessly that the insidious whispers of the 'not enough' monster implode, leaving a shimmering, self-affirming, rebellious boom in their wake.

Come along on this path, zigzagging through untamed terrain, humming with promise to revive and redefine our true nature. Let's make radical acceptance the driving force behind our personal growth and shared transformation.

Chapter Twenty-Four

The Road Less Regretted

Will Your Future Self Thank You?

"Your future self is watching you right now through memories."

— AUTHOR AND BIOMEDICAL GERONTOLOGIST AUBREY DE GREY

In the grand theater of life, where we're all playing the roles of heroes and enigmatic phantoms, there's this character waiting in the wings, ready to take center stage. It's our future self, shaped by the swirling mix of today's decisions and the relentless march of time. Looking back through a whirlwind of memories, our future self often gives our choices a thorough once-over, sometimes with a critical, maybe even a little regretful, eye. This whole dynamic between who we are now and who we'll become is summed up pretty nicely by that quote from the English author and biomedical gerontologist, Aubrey de Grey.

Life, in its infinite array of choices, presents us with what has been dubbed '*Sliding Doors* moments', a term inspired by the 1998 movie bearing the same name. The movie's all about parallel universes and how the main character's life would have taken different turns if she'd caught or missed a train, a decision as fleeting as those sliding doors closing. These moments, the choices we make or miss, create branching paths that can seriously shake up our future.

What Aubrey de Grey's getting at is that our future self is shaped by the path we're walking right now, like a web of roads splitting and merging in the wilderness of life. The choices we make or don't make in these *Sliding Doors* moments leave an imprint on our future self. So, it's like this ongoing debate: will our future self give us a high-five or shake their head in disappointment when they look back at those pivotal moments?

Navigating this 'road less regretted' business is kind of like facing those *Sliding Doors* moments head-on. It's about grabbing opportunities, challenging the status quo, embracing change, strengthening relationships, and dumping those habits that keep us stuck. Sure, it can be tough, but it promises a future self who looks back with satisfaction and gratitude.

So, here's a question to toss around when those *Sliding Doors* moments pop up: 'Is what I'm doing now something my future self will thank me for?'

It helps us make choices that match our long-term goals and values, rather than just chasing short-lived satisfaction. It's about finding purpose, satisfaction, and a sense of achievement that sticks around.

Moving from the theoretical into the tangible, the following scenarios are illustrations of how our *Sliding Doors* moments can manifest in real life and illustrate what navigating the 'road less regretted' might look like.

Take Alice, for example. She's about to graduate from college and has that classic 'what's next?' moment. She could dive into a high-paying job in the corporate world or follow her passion for environmental activism. The latter would mean tightening the purse strings but chasing deeper fulfillment.

"To be or not to be... an environmental activist?" she muses (unwittingly paraphrasing Shakespeare). But it's fitting since she's a lit major, and her predicament is pretty dramatic.

While she's weighing her choices, Alice has her own *Sliding Doors* moment. Two opportunities pop up, representing those two paths: a fat paycheck from a Fortune 500 company or an unpaid internship at an environmental organization. She remembers what Aubrey de Grey said about our future selves and asks herself, "Which path would my future self probably thank me for?"

Then there's Gary, a 45-year-old guy in the throes of a midlife crisis. He's been grinding away in a corporate job for two decades, making bank but feeling empty inside. He's daydreaming about a simpler life, maybe as a baker or a gardener.

One day, he stumbles upon an old, rundown bakery for sale. A spark of interest lights up his eyes. It's like the universe is laying out a red carpet to the life he's been yearning for. But taking that step means saying goodbye to the cushy corporate job. It's his *Sliding Doors* moment, leading him toward 'the road less regretted'.

Which is the road less regretted for Gary? The predictable, comfortable corporate job he knows inside out, or the charming bakery, full of potential but laden with uncertainty? Which choice will lead to a future self who nods approvingly, maybe even grinning knowingly, through the mirror of memories? Only time—and Gary's decision—will tell.

These examples bring us to another question: what if we make a choice and it turns out to be a dud? After all, life doesn't come with a satisfaction guarantee, nor a 'no regrets' refund policy. Regret, that nagging companion of our past choices, often looms large in the corners of our consciousness. It's the shadow of the roads we didn't take, the lives we didn't lead. Yet, regret is as much a part of our journey as the choices themselves.

Psychologists tell us that regret serves a purpose. It's a signal that our values and aspirations have evolved since we made a particular decision. Regret reminds us that we are not static beings; we grow, learn, and change. It's a testament to our capacity for self-reflection and growth.

However, it's essential to strike a balance. Dwelling too long in the realm of regret can paralyze us, preventing us from embracing new opportunities or forgiving ourselves for past missteps. It's a bit like driving forward while constantly looking in the rearview mirror—inevitably, you'll miss what's ahead.

So, as we navigate our 'road less regretted', it's worth remembering that regret, when harnessed constructively, can be a guide. It can encourage us to make choices that align more closely with our evolving values and dreams. And if we do encounter regret along the way, it's a sign that we're still growing and evolving.

Perhaps we ought to view our choices—even the ones that feel like mistakes—as steppingstones rather than stumbling blocks. This perspective could provide a safety net for our inevitable missteps. At least, that's what my future self tells me.

Whether it's Alice standing at the threshold of adult life or Gary contemplating a mid-life career change, the choices we make are bound to shape the image that our future selves will reflect on. And if we're brave enough to pick the path that resonates with our core values, we'll likely meet a future self who, while nostalgically recalling a few missed trains, wears an approving grin more often than a rueful frown.

So, how would you navigate your 'road less regretted'? Are your Sliding Doors moments pushing you towards a future self who will give you a thumbs up, or are they leading you towards a future self who might occasionally facepalm?

With greater intentionality in our choices and actions, especially during these *Sliding Doors* moments, we'll uncover increased satisfaction, well-being, and a renewed sense of purpose in forging a life that's both meaningful and fulfilling. Embracing the 'Road Less Regretted' by recognizing and acting on our *Sliding Doors* moments not only provides the opportunity to shape a better future self but allows us to reflect on our past choices without regret.

What will your journey on the 'Road Less Regretted' look like? Are your *Sliding Doors* moments crafting a script for a future self who will applaud your past choices or are they directing you towards a sequel filled with reruns of 'What if?'. Ultimately, it's your hand on the wheel, your foot on the pedal. Drive safely, but don't forget to enjoy the ride.

Chapter Twenty-Five

Wasting Time? Not On My Watch!

"Time is both free and priceless. The person you are now is a consequence of how you used your time in the past. The person you'll become in the future is a consequence of how you use your time in the present. Spend your time wisely, gamble it intrinsically and save it diligently."

— ENTREPRENEUR AND PODCASTER STEVEN BARTLETT

Time is our most precious asset, yet we seem to let it slip through our fingers like sand. As entrepreneur and podcaster Steven Bartlett wisely articulated, the person you are and will become is essentially a result of how you allocate your time. The irony is that we revere time in theory, recognizing its infinite worth, yet we squander it without remorse. We kill it with our indifference, assassinating precious moments that could be used to build, learn, and connect. We spend time carelessly, treating it like loose change, oblivious to its fleeting nature.

In the grand scheme of things, we find ourselves entangled in a ruthless battle between the urgent and the significant. The excitement of quick wins can make us forget about our long-term objectives. We sacrifice the profound for the mundane, forsaking growth and purpose for trivial pursuits.

Yet wasting time is an act of self-disrespect, a betrayal of our potential. It is an affront to the ephemeral essence of life itself. It's one thing to understand the value of time in the abstract, but it becomes all the more tangible when we witness its misuse up close and personal. Sometimes, it takes a real-world example to drive home the urgency of managing our time well. Allow me to share an experience involving my son Michael that perfectly illustrates this point.

Reflecting back to when my son Michael was in his final year of high school, he had had a major surgery and was recovering at home. Despite this, he still needed to prepare for his final exams. His best friend Brad came over to help him study. I could hear noises coming from upstairs that didn't sound anything like studying, so I went up to check on them and to offer them lunch as it was nearly noon. His bedroom door was partially open so I could hear them joking around.

As I got closer to his room, I heard Brad exclaim, "Uh oh, we're in trouble!" and Michael responded: "Don't worry, my mom's just going to ask us some questions."

I wasn't expecting that comment, and I tried really hard not to laugh. But I was glad Michael said that because that was exactly what I was going to do. I knocked on Michael's door, entered, and asked a simple question: "Are you making the best use of your time?"

Michael responded by shrugging, looking at Brad and asking: "See? I told you she was just going to ask us some questions!"

Brad turned to me, puzzled, and asked: "You're not going to get mad at us? My mother would have killed us by now!"

For me it was a no brainer. If I nagged and got angry at them, would it have taught them a lesson?

I told Brad: "At this point, you are young adults who have to make the best decisions you can. It's not up to me to force you to do well in school so you get the best possible job in a career you love. That's your responsibility, not mine. My job as a parent was to just ask the question. It's simple, really. Because at the end of the day, the way we use our time says a lot about how we value ourselves and our goals."

I asked them if they were hungry and told them there was food in the kitchen. Over lunch, we had a great conversation after which they told me (with a smile) they were going to go upstairs and hit the books. And I thought, 'How great is it that they now perceive studying as a means to an end, a path to their future?'.

It is important to explore our current relationship with time and the way we spend it. Are we prioritizing our own needs and time, and have we inadvertently handed the reins of our life over to the demands and expectations of others?

Indeed, our relationship with time is much like that of a rebellious teenager and their unexpectedly generous parent; we take it for granted, we abuse its kindness, and only when we've squandered it do we realize its value. Time, much like that tolerant parent, keeps giving while we, the petulant child, keep taking without a shred of gratitude.

Now, you're probably shaking your head, indignantly murmuring to yourself, 'Not me, I respect time'. Well, that might be true, but let's test that claim. Go ahead and pull out your recent browser history, check your smartphone screen time, or dare I suggest, the time spent crafting the perfect cat meme.

Oh, the shock and horror!

But not to worry; there's hope yet. Let's outline steps to help get our priorities straight.

Step 1: Time Trials: Time to Get Your Life in Check: What? An audit? Are you running a business here? Yes, you are the CEO of your life. Spend a week jotting down how you spend your time. You'll be surprised to see how much of it you devote to scrolling mindlessly through social media, watching random YouTube videos, or arguing with strangers online.

Step 2: Goal Gauntlet: Carve Your Path to Greatness: Now that you're a fully certified time auditor, it's time to set some goals. Ask, 'What's really important to me?'. Here's a hint: if your answer is 'Watching a panda sneeze for the hundredth time', you may need to reevaluate your life choices.

Step 3: Priority Power Play: Sorting the Gems from the Junk: Time to arrange your goals in order of importance. If 'become a master guitarist' is more important than 'beat the high score on Candy Crush,' then you know what to do. You've got to shove Candy Crush down the ladder of priorities.

Step 4: Time Tug-of-War: Dance with Balance, But Don't Starve the Beast: Now, don't just starve Candy Crush completely, unless you're a time management monk. The key is balance. Assign more time to your high-priority goals and less to low-priority ones. Remember, 'all work and no play make Jack a dull boy'. Or a bored guitarist.

Step 5: Habitual Havoc: Unleash the Consistency Beast: Consistency is your best friend. Make your time investment a habit. Routine can be boring, but it's also the stuff that success stories are made of.

Step 6: Reassess Rebellion: Stay Flexible, Crush Curveballs: Think you're done? Ha! Good one. The journey to mastering time is never-ending. Always reassess your goals and the time you allocate to them. Stay flexible and adapt to life's curveballs.

Step 7: The Mindset Makeover: Vanquish Procrastination and Mental Barriers By now, you might be wondering, "These steps seem fantastic, but what if my own mind becomes the enemy of my time? What if procrastination grips me like a vice?" Well, you're not alone; even the best of us falters when it comes to mental roadblocks. Here's the trick: confront these barriers head-on.

1. **Unearth the Root**: Sometimes procrastination isn't just laziness; it's a sign of an underlying issue—perhaps fear of failure or even success. Get to the heart of why you're putting things off.

2. **Small Wins**: Overwhelmed by a gargantuan task? Break it into smaller, manageable tasks. Completing these will give you the confidence to tackle the bigger picture.

3. **Accountability Arsenal**: Share your goals with someone you trust. Knowing that someone else is aware of your objectives can add an extra layer of accountability that may just push you into action.

4. **The 5-Minute Rule**: If you find it hard to start, commit to doing the task for just five minutes. More often than not, you'll find that getting started is the

toughest part, and once you're in it, you'll continue far beyond the initial five minutes.

5. **Reset and Recharge**: Last, don't underestimate the power of a mental reset. A short walk, a quick meditation session, or even a brief nap can recharge your mental batteries, giving you the stamina to vanquish time-wasting tendencies.

So, don your mental armor and wield these strategies like a knight brandishing a sword against the looming dragons of procrastination and self-doubt.

There you have it, a seven-step guide to stop disrespecting your time and start harnessing its power. It won't be easy. You'll probably stumble and fall and might even end up watching that sneezing panda again but keep at it. You owe it to your future self.

In the end, the harsh reality remains: time (unlike a surprisingly patient parent) is non-renewable. So, you could either be a 'timewaster' binge-watching that next Netflix series or you could rise to the rank of a 'time-master', seizing your life second by second. Your call. But remember, unlike Netflix episodes that you can revisit, 'time is non-renewable'.

Chapter Twenty-Six

Endgame, Deconstructed

Making It Happen

"People think dreams aren't real just because they aren't made of matter, of particles. Dreams are real. But they are made of viewpoints, of images, of memories and puns and lost hopes."

— WRITER NEIL GAIMAN

Dream big, right? We've all got ambitions, dreams, and those pie-in-the-sky wishes. But let's face it, if you're only dreaming and not doing, you're pretty much just a daydreamer. It's not about just wishing on a star; it's about lacing up your boots and starting the trek toward it.

So, you've got that nagging voice in your head, 'Plan (B)e the Change', that's like your mental coach. It's that persistent itch you've got to scratch—it's telling you to wake up, smell that ambition brewing, and get moving.

But waking up isn't just about opening your eyes, right? It's tuning in to what you really want and understanding what it'll take to get it. Think of yourself as the conductor of your own life's orchestra—you've got to know when to bring in the violins and when to let the drums roll.

Now, there's no backup plan here. No safety nets. So what? That shouldn't stop you from diving deep into the unknown territories of your dreams and desires. Heck, even if your plans aren't as precise as a Swiss watch, who cares?

Your determination, solid as a rock, is what pushes you to explore your own inner world. Every step you take, every mistake or win you make, propels you forward. It's like life's own way of giving you a nudge—or sometimes a shove.

Ever think about why Isaac Newton didn't just sit there after that apple bonked him on the head? He got to work. Or consider a runner—you can dream about that finish line all you want, but you've got to move those legs to make it there.

So, hold up. What's stopping us? Why do we sometimes freeze up instead of acting on our desires? Often, it's good ol' fear. Yeah, we're scared of failing, of what people will say, or even—get this—of actually succeeding. Weird, right?

I've seen it time and again over the years: people come so close to grabbing what they want and then—bam—they pull back. It's like they get stage fright just before the grand finale.

How do we get past this hang-up? One trick is to break your big dreams down into bite-sized pieces. Picture your goal as a massive puzzle; start putting it together one piece at a time, and suddenly it doesn't seem so daunting.

Take Emily, for example. Emily, a marketing manager, refused to let her day job dampen her fierce passion for environmental conservation. She was determined to make a significant impact on the environment while excelling in her professional life. Through strategic planning and unwavering dedication, Emily emerged as a force to be reckoned with, unleashing her inner environmental warrior without compromising her career.

1. **Time Mastery and Prioritization:** Emily demonstrates mastery over her time. She evaluates her schedule carefully, identifying precious hours she can dedicate to environmental activism outside of her day job. By carving out specific time slots during evenings, weekends, and lunch breaks, she maximizes her impact during these dedicated moments.

2. **Unleashing Weekends of Impact:** Weekends become the battleground for Emily's environmental superhero powers. She seeks out volunteer

opportunities, high-energy events, and powerful workshops that align with her day job schedule. With her unwavering passion, she generates a seismic impact that leaves everyone in awe.

3. **Online Platforms—Where Emily Reigns Supreme:** Emily harnesses the power of online platforms with expertise. She embraces social media as an agent for change, using captivating posts to engage her audience and lead them towards a greener world. Her blog becomes a fortress of knowledge, inspiring others to rise up and join the fight.

4. **Remote Advocacy—Breaking Barriers, No Matter Where She Is:** Emily defies location barriers by engaging in remote advocacy efforts. Fearlessly attending virtual meetings and webinars hosted by top environmental organizations, she signs online petitions with just a few clicks, becoming an unstoppable force in the digital realm, all while enjoying her morning coffee.

5. **The Fearless Faction—Teaming Up with Office Rebels:** Emily seeks out fellow office rebels who share her burning desire for environmental change. Together, they ignite conversations, organize behind the scenes meetings, and rally their colleagues within the workplace. Their collective power creates a noticeable shift, leaving a lasting impact that permeates the very walls of their office.

6. **Personal Development—Fueling the Fire Within:**
   Emily fuels her inner fire through continuous
   personal development. She devours powerful
   podcasts during her commute, absorbing
   knowledge, and inspiration. Challenging the
   status quo through thought-provoking books and
   following trailblazers who fearlessly lead the charge,
   her mind becomes a force to be reckoned with,
   intensifying her activism.

7. **Goals—Setting the World Ablaze, One Step at a
   Time:** Emily sets audacious goals that even the
   fiercest advocates would find daunting. However,
   she understands the importance of balance and
   self-care. Setting realistic targets, she ensures she
   can conquer them without sacrificing her sanity.
   Emily is in it for the long haul, recognizing that even
   small steps forward can ignite a blaze capable of
   changing the world.

By deconstructing her environmental activism dreams and
harnessing her time and resources with fierce prowess,
Emily unleashes her inner warrior. With impeccable time
management, dominance in the online realm, finesse
in remote advocacy, strategic collaborations, continuous
personal growth, and bold goal setting, Emily leaves
an indelible mark on the planet. Brace yourself for the
unstoppable force that is Emily.

As another example Debra had a burning desire to start the Rise-and-Shine baking empire. A spirited dreamer with a hunger for something more, she's always had a rebellious spirit and a secret desire to rule the baking world. But entrepreneurship? That seemed scarier than facing a horde of hangry customers. So, armed with her apron and more than a pinch of self-doubt, Debra embarked on a journey of self-discovery and doughy delights.

1. **Identifying Passion and Expertise:** Debra took a long, hard look at her life and realized that her true calling was... [drumroll, please]... baking. Yes, she had the superpower of creating mouthwatering pastries that made anyone buckle at the knees. Armed with her rolling pin and a lot of determination, she decided to channel her culinary expertise into opening a bakery.

2. **Market Research and Target Audience:** Debra didn't just wing it; she went into full-on detective mode, stalking other bakeries in the area and questioning random people on the street. She even used her invisibility cloak (i.e., online surveys) to understand the local demand for baked goods. After hours of sleuthing, she discovered that there was a niche craving for artisanal, organic pastries.

3. **Developing a Business Plan:** Debra may be a rebel, but she's no wild child. She knew she needed a game plan to conquer the baking kingdom. Fueled

by endless cups of coffee and her trusty laptop, she masterfully crafted a business plan that would make even the most seasoned entrepreneurs tremble with envy. She defined her mission, plotted her product offerings, and strategized her way to profitability.

4. **Acquiring Necessary Skills and Knowledge:** Debra didn't just rely on her baking prowess alone. She knew that to stand out from a sea of aprons, she needed to improve her skills. Debra attended baking courses and workshops on small business management. She even recruited a secret league of mentors to guide her through the risky path of entrepreneurship. Armed with her newfound knowledge, she was ready to dominate the baking game and leave her competition in the dust.

5. **Obtaining Funding and Resources:** Debra didn't have a money tree growing in her backyard (bummer, right?). She had to hunt down every possible way to fund her baking empire. She considered everything from bank loans to crowdsourcing campaigns. With her trusty pitch deck in hand, she burst through the gates of investors, showcasing her vision, and securing the dough (pun intended). She even used her super networking skills to find the freshest ingredients and the most reliable equipment vendors in town.

6. **Setting Milestones and Taking Action:** Debra

wasn't one to back down from a challenge. She
turned her overwhelming dream into bite-sized
milestones and tackled them head-on. From finding
the perfect location to navigating the bureaucratic
maze of permits and licenses, nothing could stand
in her way. Armed with determination, she crafted
a visually appealing storefront and cooked up a
marketing strategy that would make Gordon Ramsay
proud. One whisk, one cake at a time, she made her
dream a reality.

7. **Adaptation and Growth:** Debra knew that even
   a baking maverick like herself needed to adapt
   and grow. She listened to her customers' every
   word (well, most of them) and adjusted her menu
   accordingly. With the power of social media and
   community events, she built a loyal army of pastry
   enthusiasts. Debra's bakery became the hottest spot
   in town, and her empire continued to rise like a
   perfectly baked brioche. She embraced change, rode
   the waves of success, and never settled for anything
   less than perfection.

In Debra's case, she climbed the ladder of success fearlessly,
expanding her business progressively and leaving a lasting
imprint on the baking world. She began by deconstructing
her endgame and methodically elevated it to new heights,
making her mark with each step along the way.

Now, let's take stock of where we are, appreciating the smaller joys in life, the tiny miracles that often go unnoticed. If we fixate solely on the endgame, we may inadvertently overlook the beauty of the process. It's like watching a movie and only caring about the end credits, disregarding the plot twists, romance, action scenes, and even the popcorn that gets stuck in our teeth.

And let's not miss out on the true essence of this journey. It's time to roll up our sleeves, break a sweat, and seize the opportunity. The endgame is just that: the end. What truly matters is the journey itself, the path we tread, and the risks we take along the way. It encompasses valleys and mountains, trials, and tribulations, leading us through a thrilling ride and a beautiful mess.

The answer to our deepest longings lies in the actions we take to achieve them. After all, a goal without a plan is nothing more than a wish and, as the adage goes, wishes alone cannot pave the path to our dreams. What endgame are you going to deconstruct?

A goal is a dream with a deadline, and deadlines don't wait for anyone. The clock is ticking, so let's not wait for the right moment; let's make the moment right.

Don't get me wrong; patience is valuable. It's the slow simmer that turns ingredients into a gourmet meal. But there's a fine line between patience and procrastination, one we cross far too easily. Yes, we must be patient enough to see our efforts come to fruition but vigilant enough not to let our dreams whither in the soil of stagnation.

Now, you might be asking: 'How do I navigate this complex terrain? How do I sustain momentum without burning out?'

Well, I'm glad you asked.

- **Tending the Garden of Ambition:** Just like a garden requires constant tending, watering, and care, so does your ambition. And let's not forget the weeds—distractions and fears that creep in quietly. Pull them out before they choke your dreams. Keep the garden of your ambition fertile with continual learning, nurture it with varied experiences, and see your efforts bloom into success.

- **Harvesting the Low-Hanging Fruits:** Sometimes, the initial steps in your journey might seem insignificant. But remember, every mighty oak was once a simple acorn. Start with attainable tasks, build your confidence, and then tackle the bigger, more intimidating goals.

- **Find Your Tribe, Share the Vibe:** Your journey will inevitably be dotted with challenges. During these times, lean on your support system—those who believe in your vision as much as you do. There's power in collective energy, an intangible force that can elevate you when you're sinking and cheer you on when you're winning.

- **Facing the Demons:** Every hero's journey comes with its set of villains—the naysayers, the skeptics, the inner critic. Face them head-on, understand the root of their existence, and dismantle their arguments with the sword of your convictions. You are the hero of your story; you set the narrative.

- **Grit, Grind, and Go:** Perseverance will be your most loyal companion. When you're pushing through late nights, fueled only by the intoxicating aroma of your dreams, remember why you started in the first place. Your willpower is a renewable resource; recharge it with reminders of your purpose and the difference you aim to make.

So, let's revisit the endgame. It's easy to fixate on it as the ultimate climax, but remember, the most enriching experience is the journey—every challenge navigated, every milestone achieved, and every lesson learned along the way. If 'Plan (B)e the Change' resonates with you, recognize that change isn't something on the distant horizon; it's shaped by the actions you take right here, right now.

Think of your dream as a screenplay waiting to be brought to life. As the director of your story, you have the power to call 'Action!' and change the course of your life. So, savor the journey, embrace the struggle, and become the inspiration for someone else's 'Plan (B)e the Change'.

While it's often said that life is more about the journey than the destination, the transformation we undergo in the process is equally vital. Your Plan B, or rather your Plan 'Be', is not a fallback; it's a versatile strategy toolkit. It equips you to be resilient, adaptable, and agile, ensuring you stay focused on your ultimate goal through every twist and turn.

By acting on the 'Plan (B)e the Change' mantra, you're not merely aspiring for a lofty ideal; you're making it a lived reality through every step and decision. It's not about settling for less but aspiring for more, especially when challenges arise. You're not alone on this journey; each of us is crafting a unique story, bound together by the common thread of change.

So, let's make our ambitions more than daydreams. Let's make our aspirations real through our actions and embrace the trek with resilience and hope. Because that's how we don't just plan for change; we become it.

Chapter Twenty-Seven

Digging Out of a MinkHole

"Sometimes we create our own traps. We build luxurious mink holes of comfort, only to realize that they are cages."

—AUTHOR, SPEAKER, AND EXECUTIVE COACH DONNA KARLIN

Imagine falling into a fur-lined rat hole. Sounds strange, right? But bear with me. Imagine that this rat hole is covered with the softest mink fur you can think of, making it irresistibly comfortable. At first, it might seem like a luxurious retreat. But, in reality, it's still a rat hole—a trap that lures you in with its false comfort, only to keep you stuck.

This is what I like to call a 'mink hole', a term I often use when lecturing on my Shadow Coaching® methodology,

illustrating some of the 'code' terms I use with clients. We
have this unique ability to dig ourselves into emotional
and psychological mink holes—self-made sanctuaries that
become our cages.

Don't get me wrong; these mink holes can be deceivingly
cozy. Wrapped in the fabric of habits and routines, they
might seem like the safest places on Earth. But it's
precisely within their plush walls that the real danger
lurks—walls we've built with bricks made of stubbornness,
self-righteousness, and an intense desire to be right.

Now, let's get into the nitty-gritty. These mink holes aren't
just spaces or circumstances; they're emotional landscapes,
too. Ever had that moment where you double down in an
argument just to prove you're right? You feel temporarily
powerful, but all you're really doing is digging that mink hole
deeper.

For example, I once walked into a client's office and
was immediately struck by a palpable tension. My client,
who's usually the epitome of calm, was uncharacteristically
harsh with his assistant. The atmosphere was thick with
discomfort. When the assistant left the room, the client
turned to me and admitted: "I fell deep into my mink hole
this time, didn't I?"

The acknowledgment was a start, and to his credit, he took
the next step and made amends.

"I need to apologize," he said resolutely, stepping out to find his assistant. When he returned, the look on his face was one of mixed relief and introspection.

"We talked about it," he told me. "I made it clear that my behavior was not excusable, mink hole or not."

That's what it's about—taking that initial realization and turning it into action.

"The key now is identifying what leads you into that mink hole to begin with," I advised him.

He nodded, his face reflecting the gravity of this newfound self-awareness.

"That's my next challenge," he conceded.

Next, let me tell you about this overachiever I knew. Whenever things didn't pan out, she'd be her own worst critic, really deep diving into her mink hole. She thought beating herself up was her one-way ticket to the top, but it only kept her stuck in a loop of worry and doubt.

Then, she hit the pause button. Faced with yet another hiccup, she treated herself like she would a best friend—with a dose of kindness and understanding. Guess what? It was a game-changer. Her mindset improved, and she found it easier to face her challenges head-on. She went from being her own worst enemy to her own best ally.

So, empathy and compassion aren't just feel-good words; they're your toolbox for life improvement. A smidge of self-compassion can make the real difference between staying glued to the bottom of that mink hole and starting your ascent.

Before diving into the psychological mechanics, it's crucial to note that recognizing your triggers can be a lifesaver. What leads you into your mink hole in the first place? Is it stress? Certain people or situations? This understanding serves as your first tool in the 'avoiding self-made traps' toolkit.

Having recognized our tendency to create mink holes, and trust me, that's half the battle won, it's time to develop strategies to break free. Let's roll up our sleeves and get into the action plan, shall we? No one escaped a mink hole by just staring at it, right?

Step 1: Map It Out

Grab a pen and paper—or hey, your phone's note app works too—and jot down specific triggers and situations where you find yourself tumbling into your mink hole. Think of it as your "mink hole map." This map can help you recognize when you're at the edge, teetering dangerously close to another fall.

Step 2: Seek Alternatives

For each trigger or situation on your map, brainstorm alternatives. Let's say one of your triggers is stress from work. Instead of going into isolation or denial mode, could you perhaps go for a brisk walk? Maybe call a friend? The idea is to have a go-to list of healthier responses.

Step 3: Accountability Buddy

Find someone you trust and share your action plan with them. This person will be your 'mink hole watchdog'. When they see you inching towards a trap, they can give you a gentle nudge (or a hard push, depending on what you need) in the right direction.

Step 4: Practice Mindfulness

You've probably heard this one before, but it's a gem. Mindfulness techniques like deep breathing or focused attention can act like a 'pause button', giving you the momentary break you need to choose a different path. This is your 'anti-digging' tool if you will.

Step 5: Reward Yourself

Every time you avoid a mink hole, give yourself a pat on the back. Seriously, reward yourself with something—maybe your favorite treat or an extra episode of that show you're binge-watching. Positive reinforcement works wonders.

Step 6: Forgive and Move On

Look, we're all human, and mink holes are seductive places. If you find yourself back in one, don't beat yourself up. Use it as an opportunity to learn and adapt your strategy for the next time around.

Step 7: Revisit and Revise

Life changes, and your mink hole triggers might too. Make it a point to revisit your map and strategies every once in a while. Tweak them as needed. Adaptability is your best friend here.

Ever wonder why we find it so easy—almost comforting—to settle into habits or mindsets that ultimately trap us? Well, there's more to it than just 'human nature'. It's a little journey through psychology, though let's not get too tangled in jargon. The idea here is to understand why we dig ourselves into mink holes, even when a part of us knows better.

Now, speaking of knowing better, why do we crave the familiar like it's comfort food? Our brains are wired to seek out familiarity; it's kind of a survival thing. When we stick to routines or beliefs with which we're comfortable, our brain can focus on other stuff because it doesn't have to work hard to adapt or change. It's like driving on a road you've traveled a hundred times—you can practically do it in your sleep. That comfort zone becomes our own little mink hole.

So, if familiarity feels so good, what's the deal with stubbornness? I mean, it feels empowering in the moment, right? When life gets hectic or stressful, feeling like you're in control of something can be a big relief. You dig your heels in, refusing to budge on an issue or a routine, and it gives you a temporary feeling of mastery. But just like biting into fool's gold, that sense of control is often an illusion. The only thing you're controlling is your descent deeper into that mink hole.

Okay, but there must be some kind of payoff for sticking to the same old, same old, isn't there? There's a psychological payoff to being stubborn or sticking to routines, and it often comes in the form of emotional safety. By never venturing outside what we know, we avoid the risk of failure or embarrassment. In the short term, it feels like a win. But here's the catch: emotional safety is not the same as emotional growth or well-being.

You might be wondering, 'Why should I care? I'm comfortable and safe, aren't I?'. What's the downside of all this comfort and emotional safety?

Simple. It holds you back.

If you're always opting for the familiar route, you'll never discover the other amazing paths that might take you somewhere even better. Plus, you're also depriving yourself of essential life skills like resilience, adaptability, and the ability to deal with failure. Trust me, the more you avoid these experiences, the more overwhelming they become when you can't dodge them any longer.

Now, have you ever felt isolated in your mink hole? Stubbornness can isolate you. It may feel empowering to stand your ground, but when you refuse to consider other perspectives or needs, you end up alienating people. That's another deep dig into the mink hole, and it's a lonely place to be.

And let's not forget the trap of equating being 'right' with being happy. It's easy to fall into that particular comfort zone in your mink hole, but it's also an illusion. If you're more invested in being right than in understanding others or growing, you're missing out on a vital part of human interaction and self-improvement.

So, there you have it. This is why we find ourselves digging mink holes, wrapping up in the comfort they provide, even when that comfort is, at best, a double-edged sword. Recognizing these psychological trappings is the first step in grabbing that shovel and starting the climb out.

Now that we've gained some clarity about why we find ourselves in these mink holes and have developed some strategies to climb out, let's look at the bigger picture. It's about not just individual actions but also a mindset shift. We've already talked about identifying what triggers your descent into these self-made traps. Armed with that knowledge, the real work begins—it's time to actively engage with your 'avoiding self-made traps' toolkit and make conscious choices.

Next, have a game plan. This could be as simple as taking deep breaths, stepping away for a moment, or engaging in a bit of mindfulness. It's about reclaiming control.

Empathy comes next. Think of it as your secret sauce for cooling down heated moments. And hey, don't be too hard on yourself. Everyone stumbles; the trick is turning those trips into dance moves—aka learning experiences.

So, what's next? Look, mink holes can manifest in all areas of life—in dead-end jobs, stagnant relationships, and even in the comfort of routine. But recognition is the first step to freedom. It's your signal to change, to grow, to break away from the allure of comfort.

So, what's the plan? A bold leap into the unknown, challenging the comfort zones we've snuggled into. But let's pause for a sec. Have you ever wondered how staying in your mink hole could be affecting other parts of your life? No (wo)man is an island, right?

You see, the thing about these mink holes is that they don't just exist in a vacuum; they impact everything around you. Take relationships, for instance. Let's say you're so invested in being right all the time that you stop listening to your partner. What happens? Resentment builds up, doesn't it? Over time, your unwillingness to step out of your comfort zone strains the relationship, maybe even breaks it.

And what about your job? Picture this: you're so used to doing things 'your way' that you're not open to new approaches or technologies. What's the outcome? Well, in an ever-changing business landscape, adaptability isn't just a buzzword; it's survival. Staying in your mink hole means getting left behind. Before you know it, your performance is slipping, and you're questioning your job security.

Now, let's not skip the elephant in the room—your mental health. Stagnation has a way of feeding anxiety and depression. When you're not growing, when you're not challenging yourself, it's easy to slip into a mindset where you feel stuck, which is never good for your well-being. The less you venture out, the more you reinforce the walls of your mink hole, making them harder to escape.

So, yeah, the stakes are high. It's not just about you but it's also about your connections to people and the opportunities that could be knocking at your door. Ignoring them could mean a lifetime of regrets, and I don't know about you, but that's not a risk I'm willing to take.

In essence, the mink hole is not just a metaphor but a reflection of the complex web of emotional, psychological, and practical decisions we navigate every day. These self-made traps don't just limit us—they ripple out, affecting our relationships, our career, and our mental health.

Digging ourselves out isn't just an act of personal liberation—it's a radical form of self-improvement that empowers us to live richer, more meaningful lives. As we climb out of these plush pits of our own making, what awaits us is not just the absence of confinement but the presence of endless possibilities.

Time to talk action. When you finally claw your way out of that mink hole, what you find on the other side is growth, potential, and a richer, more fulfilling life. And trust me, that's a climb worth making.

Chapter Twenty-Eight

Assumption or Fact?

"Assume nothing, question everything."

— AMERICAN AUTHOR JAMES PATTERSON

In James Patterson's 1997 book *Cat and Mouse*, a certain wisdom emerges that could be more than just an intriguing idea; it could be our guide to better discernment. This isn't just a catchy phrase to toss around on social media. Rather, it's a principle that urges us to act like detectives, critically examining every assumption that poses as a fact. We do this not just for the thrill of mental exercise but to navigate life more wisely and guard against the spread of misinformation.

Here's my bold claim: If we base our decisions or determinations on assumptions, those assumptions will become true. I know it's a strong statement, but I've witnessed how often it happens. The assumption will cling to us, come rain or shine, until that assumption becomes our reality. It sounds like a horror story from the Twilight Zone, doesn't it?

So, I ask: 'Assumption or fact?'. A seemingly innocent question that's a potent antidote to cognitive bias. It invites us into the open court of objectivity, insisting that we interrogate our beliefs, asking, 'Do you swear to tell the truth, the whole truth, and nothing but the truth?'. It's humbling to realize that our truths might be just shy of honest. But it's also liberating, like breaking free from the self-imposed prison of preconceptions and emerging into the bright daylight of clear, unbiased thinking.

Let me share a personal anecdote that illustrates the consequences of acting on assumptions. I was talking to a past classmate of mine from school, Sharon, whom I had kept in touch with over the years, and I asked her if she was going to attend our high school reunion. When she confirmed that she was attending, I made plans to meet up with her just outside the doors to the gym so we could walk through the crowds together and see who we recognized.

I asked Sharon if there were specific people she wanted to see after all this time.

She replied: "I can't WAIT to see Tina. She was really bitchy and ignored me. Whenever I'd pass her and her cliquey group, they would whisper and chuckle about something, making me feel insignificant. I want to see her and let her know just how well I've done in life and see what she's made of herself!"

As we scanned the room, Sharon spotted Tina standing in the middle of the room talking to a few other classmates.

She grabbed my arm and exclaimed: "Let's go!"

We walked over to Tina, and before she could say a word, Sharon blurted out: "There you are! I was wondering if you were going to be here!"

Before Sharon could say anything else or accuse Tina of treating her badly throughout high school, Tina responded: "Good to see you! I always wondered why you didn't talk to me in high school. I always thought you didn't like me and was hoping to finally find out why."

Sharon was floored. She didn't know how to respond.

After a few seconds of silence, she answered sheepishly: "I thought it was the other way around. I always believed you didn't like me and were talking about me behind my back."

Now it was Tina's turn to be discombobulated.

Both Sharon and Tina had acted on assumptions. Each assumed the other didn't like them and reacted instead of seeking the truth. The three of us found a quiet corner to talk, catch up, and address the other assumptions that had developed over time.

Tossing out the question, 'Assumption or fact?' is akin to tossing a wrench into the cogs of our decision-making machinery. It demands a hard stop and an intense deep dive into the murky waters of our preconceptions. It's a self-imposed audit, urging us to scrutinize the integrity of our perspectives before they solidify into unchangeable judgments.

But this interrogation doesn't stop with us. It's a gateway to dynamic dialogue, a signal flare announcing our willingness to entertain differing viewpoints. It's less of a chess match where we calculate our next move to outmaneuver our opponent and more of a dance, where partners constantly adapt to each other's rhythm. This dance of open discourse can make all the difference in building trust and cultivating a symphony of constructive conversations. After all, who wouldn't want to dance their way through misunderstandings and assumptions to the tune of unfiltered truths?

Let me share another example highlighting the consequences of acting on assumptions. This one involves my client, Daniel, who held the position of Vice President at his company for many years. When a new President joined the organization, he took his time to familiarize himself with the critical issues and how they were being addressed.

About a month into the President's tenure, Daniel was called upstairs for a last-minute Executive Committee meeting. As Daniel's Shadow Coach, I was invited to accompany him to the meeting, give feedback and support, and pick up on details he might miss. Throughout the proceedings, I observed subtle cues, unspoken concerns, and underlying tensions, providing valuable insights. My objective was to offer Daniel a fresh perspective, maximize his leadership potential, and enhance his understanding of the situation. This enabled informed decision-making and a deeper awareness of the organizational landscape.

After the meeting, we came back to his office to discuss what had occurred. The first thing he said was: "I want you to help me find a new job."

This statement surprised me, considering he had been working with this organization for years and had previously enjoyed his work and his colleagues.

I asked him: "What? Where is this coming from?"

To which he replied: "The boss doesn't value me at all and thinks I have nothing worthwhile to add to the team, so it's time I left."

I looked at him and responded: "So, did he actually say that he thinks you're an idiot with no value add to the organization?"

(This is what I call a 'shocking them into awareness' question.)

That got his attention! (I'm not subtle with my clients.)

"No! He didn't say that!" he answered.

"So, is that an assumption or fact?" I asked. And then I continued: "This meeting was about an overseas issue. Did you say anything at the meeting, or did anyone ask you to weigh in? Did any of it involve the work you do?"

"No," he answered.

I continued: "So, let's recap for a moment. You didn't say anything, mostly because it didn't involve your area. He didn't hear your perspective on the issue. The President has been here for only one month. So, if he hasn't heard anything from you, how has he had an opportunity to get a sense of you, your ideas, or what you can contribute?"

We then discussed what he could do to ensure that the President would truly get to know him and his contributions. We talked about the pitfalls of making assumptions and acting on them, which was what he was doing at that moment.

A few days later, while I was working with Daniel, he received a call summoning him to the President's office for a meeting. Although I usually accompanied him on such occasions, I decided to let him go alone this time. I wanted him to self-observe and later report back to me with his conclusions. During our discussion, Daniel expressed his aspirations to pursue a position in the field overseas and requested the President's support in achieving this goal.

There would be no assumptions or waiting to be noticed; he intended to make a direct request, ensuring the President understood his intentions, the duration of his stay, and the objectives he aimed to accomplish.

He came back about an hour later, filled with excitement.

"I aced that meeting! I told the President my views on what we were doing and possible ways of doing it better and how my area could support that. I also told him I wanted to be transferred to a field position to work overseas for a while and asked for his support. AND I GOT IT!" he said excitedly.

Then he shared how challenging assumptions could have prevented movement in his career path and how challenging those assumptions made all the difference.

Just like Daniel's experience demonstrated the positive impact of challenging assumptions on one's career, the following example highlights the importance of questioning our assumptions.

The case involved an organization run by a former student. She contacted me for help with a situation at her workplace.

She asked: "I need some consulting on a situation at my work. Can you help me out?"

"Of course," I responded. "What's going on?"

"Well, there seems to be tension between the Chairman of the Board and the CEO, along with the Senior Legal

Counsel and his second. The CEO and Chairman want to fire the lawyers, but the Chief Counsel wants to keep them on board."

"Okay, I see. Do you have any details on why they want to fire the lawyers?"

"I don't have much information, but I can put you in touch with the Chief Counsel."

"Sure, let's do that," I said. "I want to learn more before agreeing to consult on this."

A few days later, I spoke with the Chief Counsel and asked: "What's going on exactly?"

The Chief Counsel replied: "The CEO and Chairman both want to fire the Senior Counsel and his second, but I believe they are vital to the organization and do amazing work. However, I'm not sure why the CEO and Chairman want to let them go. They just told me they're upset with them."

"Upset with them for what?" I asked.

"I'm not sure."

"I need to talk to the CEO and Chairman individually and in person. I want to hear what they have to say."

I flew in to meet with the Chairman first. When I asked him for more context, his first question was: "What did the CEO tell you?"

"Nothing," I replied. "I haven't met with him yet. You were the first one available. What happened that made you want to fire these two people?"

"I'm not sure, but I know they did something to anger the CEO, so they should go."

The same thing happened when I subsequently met with the CEO and asked: "So, what happened to the point where you want to let go of two valuable employees?"

"They angered the Chairman, who lost patience with them, and they just have to go."

When I finally got down to the crux of the matter, it turned out that the CEO and Chairman were upset with the lawyers for acting 'too lawyer-like'. The CEO and Chairman felt like they were being spoken down to, and the CEO had an added issue with the second lawyer's bowtie, which irked him for reasons he couldn't explain. (And you thought a hard time with the boss's orthopedic shoes was a one-off!) However, when I asked whether the lawyers were competent and had the company's best interests at heart, the CEO admitted that they were.

"So, what's the problem then?" I asked.

He couldn't give me an answer.

I probed further: "But are they competent and do they have the company's best interests at heart?"

"Of course," they both said.

The Chairman also informed me that he was relatively new in his position.

I asked him: "Have you met one-on-one with each of these lawyers to let them know what you need from them?"

"Well, no. Not yet," he answered.

No one is clairvoyant, and in this case, both the Chairman and the CEO were angry at the lawyers for not fulfilling their needs, even though they hadn't communicated what those needs were. It took just a couple of conversations to get to the root of the problem and save the lawyers' jobs. Each of them had made assumptions about the other's anger and were reacting without seeking clarification.

This case serves as a reminder that even high-ranking individuals within organizations are not immune to acting on assumptions. Despite being the top decision-makers, the Chairman and CEO fell into the trap of making judgments without seeking clarification, just like any other human being, highlighting our tendency to jump to conclusions based on limited information or personal biases, regardless of one's position or authority.

I hope this realization provides you with a valuable lesson about the importance of effective communication and open dialogue in any professional setting. It underscores the need for clear expectations, open channels of communication, and the willingness to address concerns directly rather than relying on assumptions. Regardless of our roles or positions, we should always strive to foster a culture of transparency, where misunderstandings can be resolved through meaningful conversations rather than allowing assumptions to dictate our actions.

Assumptions may serve as a starting point for understanding, but they should not harden into unquestioned beliefs. So how can we learn to identify and question assumptions? By unmaking the hidden assumptions and learning to think like mavericks. This is how:

Step 1: Question Everything (Yes, Even This)

Get used to it. We are going to start questioning everything. That piece of wisdom our grandmother dropped over a Sunday dinner? Question it. That random article about unicorn investments in the latest business journal? Question it. That heartwarming quote shared by our favorite influencer? Yep. That too. Question it.

The first thing we need to understand is that we're not on a witch-hunt for 'the truth'. We're hunting assumptions. And these sneaky operators are like subtle graffiti, spreading their mark on our thoughts unnoticed. So, let's grab our mental flashlight and start hunting.

Step 2: Detect the Hidden Assumptions

Here's the tricky part: assumptions are often cloaked in invisibility. They've been normalized, camouflaged, slipped into our daily thoughts like uninvited guests at a house party. We must learn to spot them. How? Look for statements or beliefs that seem 'obvious', 'common sense', or 'just the way things are'. When we hear these phrases, our assumption-detection alarm should blare louder than a police siren. We must pay particular attention to our own thoughts and words; we are often the most cunning saboteurs of our thinking.

Step 3: Put Our Assumptions on Trial

Once we've spotted an assumption, it's time for some judicial action. Cross-examine it. Demand evidence. Is there any proof to back up the claim? Or is it built on shaky, undocumented hearsay? Just because something has always been believed doesn't make it gospel. Remember, there was a time people 'knew' the earth was flat.

We must put that assumption in the hot seat. Ask, 'Why?'. Then ask, 'Why?' again. And then a third time. By the time we've drilled down three 'whys', we'll often find the initial assumption has evaporated like a vampire in sunlight.

Step 4: Welcome Contradiction

Let's get cozy with contradiction. Assumptions loathe it. They survive by maintaining the status quo. They thrive in echo chambers. So, let's invite dissent. Let's surround ourselves with diverse thinking. Read opinions that oppose our own. Watch films from different cultures. Discuss ideas with people who come from different walks of life.

Sure, it's uncomfortable. But remember: the comfort zone is where assumptions breed like rabbits. We need to make our minds a less hospitable place for them.

Step 5: Never Assume We're Done

Last but not least, remember this: the hunt for assumptions is a never-ending journey. Just when we think we've eliminated them, a fresh brood pops up, ready to distort our thinking. So, we must be vigilant. We need to keep our mental muscles flexed.

In this world, there are two types of people: those who assume, and those who question assumptions. Guess which ones shape the future? Questioning our assumptions fosters discovery, welcomes diverse perspectives, and paves the way for personal growth. Let's heed the counsel from James Patterson at the start of this chapter, and continue our journey marked by intellectual curiosity, rigorous inquiry, and the relentless pursuit of truth.

Chapter Twenty-Nine

Mind Revolution

Innovate or Recycle?

"The capacity to learn is a gift; the ability to learn is a skill; the willingness to learn is a choice."

— AUTHOR BRIAN HERBERT

Picture our minds: perplexing masterpieces of biology that are so full of energy, they could power a small coffee maker. Now ask: what if our minds are trapped on an endless merry-go-round of recycling ideas, behaviors, and beliefs?

Our brains are like spongy supercomputers, eager to soak up knowledge. Yet, having the hardware isn't enough; it's the software that matters. In simpler terms, just as a chef has all the ingredients but needs the right recipe, your mind has all the potential but requires the proper 'programming' to truly innovate. The question, then, is not just what you have but how you're using it.

While recycling ideas may seem safe, comfortable, familiar, and predictable, innovation is the daring motorbike ride through the thrilling curves of the unknown. It is where magic happens, boundaries are pushed, and paradigms are shattered.

We, as creatures of habit, love our patterns, routines, and mental bubble wrap. Yet, we are also adventurers, explorers, and pioneers of the possible. Every day we face the choice between staying in the comfy recliner of recycled ideas or jumping onto the roller coaster of innovation—sometimes without knowing if we meet the height requirement.

Imagine a newborn baby: a pristine canvas waiting for the fingerpaint of life to make its mark. This tiny miracle holds, within its delicate being, the extraordinary capacity to learn—an intrinsic, untamed potential with which we all enter the world.

And viewing the skill of learning as tending to a meticulously cultivated garden reveals that learning goes beyond inherent abilities. It necessitates purposeful effort, sustained dedication, and an unwavering commitment to personal growth. To foster learning, we must actively engage with new ideas, explore diverse perspectives, and embrace challenges.

The composer Ludwig van Beethoven's path to greatness offers another compelling narrative of growth through adversity. Unlike a fairy-tale ascension to the pantheon of classical music, Beethoven's story is one of relentless struggle; from grappling with his encroaching deafness to the meticulous process of transforming musical ideas into immortal symphonies. Beethoven didn't just coast on his raw talent; no, he didn't put his compositions on 'easy mode' and let auto-tune do the work. It was his unyielding will to innovate, to push boundaries, and to continue learning that truly set his life's work apart.

At the crossroads of this triad—gift, skill, and choice—emerges a profound metamorphosis: a mind revolution. With the question, 'What don't I know that I need to know?' in mind, the ever-present thirst for knowledge nudges us beyond our cerebral horizon.

Curiosity can be likened to a bold space explorer, always ready to step off the familiar terra firma and venture into the vast chasm armed with insatiable curiosity and a sense of wonder. There is a universe waiting to be discovered; a constellation of ideas, a galaxy of possibilities, a supernova of innovation.

The courage to ask, 'What don't I know?' and 'What else is out there?' is the GPS that tells us to 'continue on the route of curiosity', even when we're tempted to take the next exit to ''Dullsville'. It is a voyage not only into the depths of the world around us but also a deep dive into the unexplored expanse of our inner selves. A mind that dares to question, to probe, to wonder is a mind that grows, evolves, and innovates.

Embrace this mindset, cultivate curiosity, and dare to ask provocative questions. Witness how your world unfurls in a dazzling display of discovery and innovation. Learning isn't a straight and narrow highway. It is a winding path through the wilderness, complete with dead ends, detours, and unexpected vistas.

Now, let's delve into the diverse examples that illustrate the concept of innovation and the willingness to learn across various fields and aspects of life:

Submerge in a Sea of Insights: Delve unreservedly into a universe brimming with varied insights. Traverse through an expanse of books, articles, and academic research, transcending disciplinary confines. Engage in intellectually stimulating dialogues with individuals from all walks of life. Attend enlightening conferences, seminars, and workshops to uncover groundbreaking thoughts and methodologies.

Welcome Diversity in Thought: Embrace the dynamic mosaic of diverse perspectives. Engage earnestly with ideas that challenge your understanding, for they can be catalysts for unique innovations. Foster an inclusive space where open discourse and varied voices weave a grand tapestry of collective wisdom.

Failure—Your Ladder to Triumph: Think of failure as the universe's way of telling you there's room for improvement—it's like the autocorrect feature for your life choices. Each misstep is a mini seminar in the school of hard knocks, complete with free life lessons. So go ahead, earn those metaphorical bruises and detours, and turn them into your steppingstones to brilliance. Remember, in the quest for innovation, a growth mindset isn't just your best friend; it's your loyal sidekick, minus the flashy costume.

Unleash the Power of Inquiry: Questions like 'Why?' and 'What if?' are the caffeinated energy drinks that your imagination didn't know it was thirsty for.

Foster Collaborative Synthesis: Collaborate with individuals from diverse fields to knit an intricate web of innovation. Let each discipline contribute its unique insights, blending harmoniously to unlock unprecedented perspectives. Harness the dynamism of interdisciplinary collaboration where varied ideas meet, erasing boundaries and propelling us towards untapped frontiers of growth and discovery.

Harbor a Sanctuary for Innovation: Champion creativity as the forefront of your efforts. Cultivate an environment where risk-taking and experimentation are lauded. Allow ingenious ideas to emerge without the fear of judgment. Salute the courage required to pioneer into the unknown.

Court Uncertainty: Harness the rhythm of uncertainty to build forward momentum. Embrace calculated risks, transforming the unknown into an orchestra of possibilities. Develop resilience as a constant companion, nimbly adapting to new challenges and capitalizing on emergent opportunities.

The Waltz of Endless Learning: Engage passionately in the waltz of lifelong learning. Keep your skills attuned to the latest developments in your field. Participate in training programs, online courses, and workshops to broaden your intellectual horizons and stay abreast with the perpetual evolution of knowledge.

Foster a Cradle of Creativity: Cultivate an ecosystem that nurtures innovation like a thriving rainforest. Offer the fertile ground, provide the necessary resources and time, and watch innovation blossom in its full grandeur. Give a standing ovation to the rebels, the rule-breakers, and the round pegs in square holes—they're the ones writing the script while the rest of us are still looking for the playbill.

These strategies can help create an environment where curiosity ignites, and innovation takes center stage on the path of personal and collective growth.

In the realm of technology, we witness disruptive innovations brought forth by companies like Apple and Tesla. They revolutionized how we interact with technology, introducing groundbreaking products such as smartphones and electric vehicles. Through their willingness to think differently and challenge the status quo, they transformed entire industries.

In the domain of science and medicine, constant advancements driven by scientists and researchers lead to new treatments for diseases like cancer or to the rapid progress in vaccine development. These innovations arise from a relentless pursuit of knowledge, a willingness to explore uncharted territory, and the courage to challenge existing limitations.

The world of art and entertainment is another arena where innovation thrives. Filmmakers like George Lucas and James Cameron have pushed the boundaries of storytelling and visual effects, transforming the movie industry. By embracing new techniques and daring to explore unexplored territories, they have created immersive experiences that captivate audiences.

Turning our attention to business and entrepreneurship, we encounter individuals like Richard Branson (founder of Virgin Galactic) and Sara Blakely (founder of Spanx). Disrupting industries through their innovative ventures, these entrepreneurs sought out opportunities where others only saw limitations, took risks, and challenged conventional wisdom to bring about transformative change.

In the realm of social and cultural change, we find movements that have sparked revolutions. From civil rights movements to sustainable environmental movements, these examples demonstrate the power of innovation in challenging societal norms, inspiring conversations, and driving significant progress towards climate change.

These diverse examples illustrate how innovation and the willingness to learn are vital across various fields and aspects of life. When contemplating the concept of innovation and the power of learning, ask: What steps will I take today to cultivate curiosity, embrace the unknown, and embark on a journey of personal and collective growth?

Chapter Thirty

Embracing Imperfection

"Forget your perfect offering. There is a crack in everything. That's how the light gets in."

— SINGER SONGWRITER LEONARD COHEN

Perfection, in its bewitching allure, often becomes the object of our deepest yearnings. We chase after the perfect job, the perfect partnership, the perfect existence, as though these ideals are attainable. But when we pause to really look, we find that perfection is but a fleeting mirage, always just out of reach.

Cohen's quote illuminates a liberating perspective, especially in a culture so fixated on achieving an unblemished, idealized state. It invites us to reconsider our relentless quest for perfection, nudging us towards acceptance of life's inherent flaws and imperfections.

Isn't it fascinating, this human inclination to idealize perfection? We're enamored by it, even though it's an illusion. Underneath the polished surface of what we consider 'perfect' lies a recurring current of unease and dissatisfaction. A nagging sense that we are somehow incomplete or lacking. So why do we put so much energy into pursuing something that, ultimately, saps our spirit?

Perhaps we have a relationship with the term 'perfection' that is as twisted as a pretzel at a contortionist convention. We've set ourselves up for failure by holding up an unattainable standard. Like hunting for a unicorn with a butterfly net in the concrete wilderness of our urban existence—it's pretty, but impractical. There's nothing so perfect about this projection, merely another distorted image we've created in our minds. It's akin to trying to find the true North using a broken compass, one that we've been looking at all along.

Imagine you're in a baking competition, and the judges are culinary legends with taste buds sharper than a chef's knife. You've spent hours crafting what you hope will be the perfect soufflé. Every ingredient has been meticulously measured; every step executed with precision.

But as you watch it rise in the oven, you notice a slight wobble, and your heart sinks. Panic sets in as you frantically try to correct it. You're chasing the elusive 'perfect' soufflé like it's the golden ticket to a lifetime supply of chocolate. In that moment, you're so focused on perfection that you forget the joy of baking and the pleasure of savoring your creation. That quest for perfection can turn even the sweetest experiences into high-stakes, stressful endeavors.

Perfection isn't a destination; it's a journey. It isn't about eliminating every single flaw, or mastering every skill, or winning every game. It's about growth, evolution, resilience. It's about being human in a way that's utterly, beautifully flawed. When we reframe perfection as embracing the whole spectrum of our existence—our triumphs and failures, our virtues and vices, our laughter, and tears—we become the architects of our own 'perfect' realities.

In essence, Cohen's statement is a subversive rebellion against the perfection paradigm. It asks us to redefine our understanding of what it means to be perfect by pointing out that the so-called 'imperfect' parts of us are actually the most perfect aspects of our humanity. They make us unique.

They make us real. They make us 'us'.

And isn't that beautifully edgy, thought-provoking, and somewhat of a relief? What a relief to realize that perfection does not lie in its attainment but in its non-attainment! It lies in the complete and unreserved acceptance of our 'imperfections'. It's not about having all the right answers;

it's about asking the right questions such as, 'What is so perfect about this when it clearly isn't?'.

Perfection—the captivating illusion that promises faultless beauty—has a peculiar knack for ensnaring our aspirations. Be it the perfect job, the perfect romance, or the perfect existence, we ache for the complete and uncompromised. And yet, when prodded, this shimmering specter of perfection all too often disintegrates, revealing itself to be nothing more than an illusion.

To illustrate the paradox of perfection, let's peruse the canvases of Vincent van Gogh, that Dutch mastermind whose genius embellishes the hallowed halls of grand museums and art galleries. Van Gogh immersed himself in the quest for perfection, weaving magic ceaselessly with his brush. But it wasn't in the perfect portrayal of subjects where he found solace; rather, it lay in the unadorned, raw beauty that radiated from his strokes, each brimming with unapologetic passion and emotion. It was in these 'imperfections' that the true resonance of his artistic prowess lay. Van Gogh's tale underscores the paradox encapsulated within the concept of perfection.

While we chase the impeccably tailored outcomes relentlessly, it's the rough edges, the subtle discordances, that lend character, depth, and authenticity to our endeavors. In the symphony of life, an occasional offbeat note or a deliberate dissonance can stir emotions far deeper than a flawlessly executed composition. The unvarnished essence of artistry, and indeed, of humanity, is nurtured within these 'imperfections'.

This paradox resonates not only in the realm of art but also in the pursuit of knowledge. We crave final answers and a definitive comprehension of existence. But as we delve deeper into the cosmic labyrinth, we realize our understanding is but a speck within the vast expanse of the unknown. Each revelation brings new questions, complexities, and uncertainties. Our quest for perfect knowledge morphs into an acceptance of our imperfect comprehension and a thirst for deeper understanding, forever pushing the boundaries of discovery.

In our personal quest for knowledge and understanding, we encounter similar challenges in embracing imperfections. The compulsion to project a pristine facade, to veil our vulnerabilities and inadequacies, can throttle our authenticity, hindering genuine human connections.

Ironically, it's through our imperfections, our wounds, our battles, that we weave the most profound connections, engendering empathy and creating spaces for growth and comprehension.

When we are caught up chasing the mirage of a perfect existence, it's all too easy to be entranced by the carefully curated illusions of flawlessness: glossy portrayals, sculpted bodies, and seemingly perfect lifestyles. Amid this relentless quest, however, echoes a voice whispering the inconvenient truth: Imperfections are perfections when we embrace who, what, and where we are.

How can imperfections equate to perfection? How can we unearth fulfillment in our flawed existence? When we peel back the layers, we find profound wisdom. We often overlook the fact that true beauty doesn't reside in conformity, but in authenticity. We are a kaleidoscope of strengths and weaknesses, victories, and defeats, joy, and sorrow. Our 'imperfections', rather than being defects to hide, are the strokes that add texture and depth to the canvas of our lives. They are the essence of our humanity.

By embracing our imperfections, we validate our inherent worth and acknowledge the entire spectrum of our existence. Our vulnerabilities enable deeper connections with others, for our shared imperfections offer common ground. The ancient Japanese art of kintsugi, uses gold to mend broken objects and make them even more beautiful than they were before. Similarly, our scars and 'imperfections' can be transformed into sources of resilience and strength.

Moreover, our imperfections serve as adjuvants for growth and self-discovery. Missteps and blunders offer invaluable lessons, bestowing both wisdom and insight. Conversely, the pursuit of perfection often leads to stagnation and fear of failure. By embracing our imperfections, we open doors for growth, innovation, and personal evolution. In the practical realm, the wisdom of embracing imperfections becomes even more palpable.

Take Justin, a senior director, whose example exemplifies how our struggles with perfection intersect with real-life situations. By asking a question in a way that challenged his thinking, Justin's experience highlighted the transformative power of embracing imperfections and its profound impact.

When called to the new President's office, he was extremely agitated. Justin hadn't yet met the new President. His boss, who was the VP and Chief Financial Officer, was overseas and Justin was being asked to come up to the President's office alone to brief him on a current hot issue.

Justin panicked and told me all the things that could go wrong.

"He's going to want information I don't have, and I can't reach my boss right now. He's going to think I'm an idiot and that's not the impression I want to leave him with! What a horrible way to meet the President for the first time. I can't tell him a series of 'I don't knows'! What should I do?"

I asked: "What is so perfect about this when it clearly isn't?"

He was (figuratively speaking) ready to kill me, or at least give me a very stern talking-to.

"What kind of stupid question is that? NOTHING is perfect about this!"

I invited him to reconsider, to take a breath, and to revisit the question.

He calmed down for a moment and ventured: "Well, I get to meet the new President which is something someone at my level would not often have the chance to."

"Yes", I responded. "And what else is perfect?"

"Well, I can tell him some of the information and offer to get back to him with the rest once I've spoken to my boss. That would give me a second meeting and a chance for the President to get to know me better."

"Definitely." I answered. "Anything else?"

"YES!" he exclaimed. "This conversation just helped me calm down and focus and I'm ready to go. Let's go and meet with him."

The whole conversation took all of five minutes. It helped center Justin and show him a different perspective of what he originally viewed as a huge problem.

Fast forward to a few weeks later, when Justin and I found ourselves waiting at the bank of elevators. Just then, his boss approached us. She had been called to the President's office to give a report, but she wasn't ready to share it yet as it was quite complex. She wanted to ensure its accuracy before having the conversation. Justin, upon hearing this, looked at her and immediately responded: "What is so perfect about this when it clearly isn't?"

The look on her face was priceless.

Her immediate question was: "Where did THAT come from?"

He pointed to me (which appeared to be all the explanation she needed) and continued by describing the premise of the question. She smiled, nodded her head, and thanked him as it helped her get her thoughts and approach straight and ready for the meeting.

Ten years later, Justin is still using that question to help guide him through challenges in his life and career.

How can we embrace this concept? We can view the imperfect as perfect (according to us) starting with:

1. **Reality Check:** Starting each day by looking in the mirror and saying, 'I'm not perfect, and that's perfectly okay', we face the reality of our human imperfection head-on. Embracing the flawsome concept, we ask ourselves why they've been branded as such, and who's doing the branding.

2. **Decoding Failure:** Make it a habit to fail regularly. Yes, you read it right. We try new things, and when we fail—and we will—we examine the failure. What did it teach us? What did it make us feel? What can we take away from the experience that helps us grow?

3. **Raw Honesty Hour:** We gather a group of friends and have each person share an 'imperfect' part of

themselves they've been hiding, or a failure they've experienced. We listen without judgment. The aim is not to comfort or console, but to normalize the reality of imperfection.

4. **Mindful Rebellion:** Perfectionism is a societal construct, and it's time for us to rebel. We use mindfulness to embrace our entire selves, warts and all. We celebrate each scar, each wrinkle, each so-called imperfection as a mark of our unique existence.

5. **The 'Let It Be' Experiment:** We find one thing that we spend too much time perfecting—whether it's our appearance, a project at work, or an Instagram post—and we just say, 'Let it be'. We do the bare minimum. We allow it to be imperfect. We sit with the discomfort that arises and then let it pass. We embrace the reality that imperfection, in fact, holds its own unique beauty.

6. **Impromptu Speech:** We ask a friend to give us a random topic and immediately deliver a five-minute speech. The aim isn't to be eloquent, but to embrace the messiness, the stutters, the 'uhs' and 'ums' and all the imperfections that come with spontaneous speech.

7. **Graffiti Wall:** We create a space on a wall in our home or workspace where we write down or

illustrate our failures, our fears, our vulnerabilities, and all our 'imperfect' bits. We make it a living testament to our rebellion against perfectionism.

8. **Dare to Disagree:** We engage in conversations about controversial topics with an open mind. We challenge our beliefs, have healthy debates, and learn to accept the inherent 'imperfections' in everyone's perspectives.

So, what is so perfect when it clearly isn't? The answer lies in acknowledging that conventional perfection is merely an illusion. It's within the nuances, the unpredictability, and the 'imperfections' of life that we discover true beauty, true growth, and true meaning.

It's through embracing our imperfections, rather than striving for an unattainable ideal, that we embark on a journey of self-discovery, resilience, and authentic transformation.

Chapter Thirty-One

Mindful Mastery

Balancing Risks and Rewards

"The only way to make sense out of change is to plunge into it, move with it, and join the dance."

— BRITISH PHILOSOPHER, SPEAKER, AND AUTHOR ALAN WATTS

Alan Watts, as he eloquently articulated in his book, *The Wisdom of Insecurity: A Message for an Age of Anxiety* (1951) articulates making sense out of change beautifully. He reminds us that life is not meant for cautious contemplation but rather, extends an invitation for us to dance in real time with whatever comes our way.

As we set sail on this wild journey, we're faced with a smorgasbord of choices. Some are as everyday as deciding what to have for breakfast, while others are as mind-blowing as picking the next intergalactic vacation spot. Each choice carries its own superpower—the ability to shape our experiences and chisel out the path of our existence. These are the moments when we need to put on our mindfulness hats and don our finesse capes, engaging in a balancing act that's as intricate as a circus tightrope walk, helping us navigate the adventurous terrain of life's twisted trade-offs.

To unlock the secret sauce of mindful mastery, we must first give a warm embrace to the ever-changing rhythm of life. Change is the sidekick to life, always running fashionably late to the party. It moves like an unstoppable force, guiding us through life's highs and lows. The world around us is in a constant state of shuffle, and we, too, are in the metamorphosis club. We grow, we evolve, we adapt. Just as Watts so eloquently put it, life's a never-ending dance that calls for our active participation.

Allow me to illustrate the power of embracing change with a story. Imagine a quaint town named Millville nestled deep in the heart of the countryside. For generations, Millville had thrived on its traditional farming practices, with its residents finding comfort in their familiar routines.

One day, the mayor of Millville gathered the townspeople to share news that would alter the course of their lives. A new highway was set to be constructed, running right through their beloved town. At first, the news was met with shock and resistance. The townsfolk feared that this change would disrupt their idyllic lives and jeopardize the close-knit community they had cherished for years.

However, the mayor saw an opportunity for Millville to reinvent itself. He encouraged the townspeople to embrace this change as a chance for growth and progress. With a united spirit, they decided to transform their town into a bustling rest stop along the highway, welcoming travelers with open arms. New businesses sprouted up, bringing economic prosperity to Millville like never before. The town's identity evolved, but its heart remained intact.

This intricate dance calls for mindful mastery—it's like getting the hang of life's choices with a bit of wisdom and grace thrown in. We can simply ask ourselves, 'How am I dealing with all this change? Am I rolling with it or am I digging in my heels like a stubborn mule?'.

When we do this, change, which is the steady beat of life, pushes us forward. Embracing change means actively engaging with it, staying in the moment, and keeping an eye out for those unexpected twists and turns. As we get in sync with the changes around us, let's take a breather and think for a sec. We can ask, 'Am I adapting to the rhythm of change? How am I responding to life's curveballs?'.

This transformative journey also means taking risks head-on and chasing those appealing rewards. Every choice we make sends ripples through our lives. So, we should wonder, 'Do I really get what might happen because of my choices? Am

I aware of how my decisions add to the grand scheme of things in my life?'.

Embracing change isn't about surrendering lazily to fate or going mindlessly with the flow. No, it's way cooler, requiring an extraordinary level of self-awareness, sharp observation skills, and an ability to stay present in the moment. After all, it's a dance. We must move with the rhythm and tempo, with the unpredictable twists and turns with style.

And here's the real kicker: decision-making itself is quite the dance-off. Striking that sweet spot between risks and rewards is like choreographing every move. Every action has consequences, and each choice leads us closer to one destiny or another. Our choices are a big deal. This is the core of mindful mastery—understanding that even the small stuff adds up to the bigger picture.

But mindful mastery isn't about playing it safe and managing risks like an actuary. It's about tackling those risks head-on and giving them a run for their money. Risks are like the spicy jalapeños of life—they add a zing, some excitement, and that extra kick. To chase the ultimate rewards, we gotta be ready to venture into the unknown, take on the unfamiliar with a mischievous grin, and tackle life with courage, resilience, and adaptability. It's a dance that's got the essence of life written all over it.

Allow me to share a profound example of the delicate dance between risks and rewards. When my son was born partially paralyzed, the Head of Neurology at the children's hospital delivered a devastating verdict: nothing could be done. His suggestion of radical amputation as a supposed solution left me in disbelief, and I firmly refused to accept such a drastic approach.

Seeking guidance and hope, I turned to my brother, who lived in another city. With desperation in my voice, I pleaded for him to explore any possible avenues and connect me with someone who could offer a glimmer of light. He did not disappoint. He introduced me to the Chief of Pediatric Plastic Surgery at his hospital, who graciously agreed to provide a consultation.

During our meeting with this remarkable physician, he detailed that a Fellow in his department was specializing in surgical neuromuscular reconstruction. While this procedure had not been attempted before, the Fellow expressed readiness to take a daring leap and treat it as an experimental approach. The risks were clear, with my son effectively becoming a test subject. Nonetheless, the possible gains, offering him an improved shot at a high-quality life, became the pivotal point in our decision-making.

Was it the best decision? Even hindsight doesn't answer that question. It was the best decision I could make at the time. There was no way we could predict what the outcome might be.

For me, the choice was crystal clear. Despite the prospect of my son enduring 18 surgeries within his first 19 years of life—a marathon, really—I stood firm. The promise of preserving his bodily integrity, giving him the best chance at an active life filled with purpose and fulfillment, was a no-brainer. I took the plunge and signed those consent forms, knowing our journey would be challenging but that the potential rewards far outweighed the risks.

This story is a testament to the intricate interplay between risks and rewards. It illustrates how sometimes the biggest risks can lead to the most extraordinary outcomes. It's about embracing uncertainty, defying conventional wisdom, and unlocking the incredible power of the human spirit. In situations like this, where risk takes center stage and fear creeps in, it's vital to grasp the tremendous weight of the overall benefits. The scales must tip significantly in favor of rewards to even begin to balance out those daunting risks.

Now, the choices we face in our lives might not always be as dramatic as my son's story, but they're significant, nonetheless. We need to navigate the twists and turns of risk and reward, carefully weighing potential consequences against promised benefits. It's in these pivotal moments that we find the resilience and determination to push past our perceived limits and step into the dance of a lifetime.

Take, for instance, those entrepreneurs on the verge of launching their groundbreaking businesses. They embody the intricate dance of risk and reward. They navigate financial uncertainty, fierce competition, and market volatility, all while eyeing those tempting rewards like financial independence and the thrill of innovation.

Every decision, from securing a loan to building a team to reshaping their business model, puts them on the edge of significant success or failure. However, these calculated risks inch them closer to rewarding outcomes. Even failures can turn into gains, providing valuable lessons in knowledge, experience, and resilience.

Then there's that mind-blowingly talented professional dancer—a true symbol of fierce grace. Hours upon hours of sweat-soaked practice go into perfecting a single performance. She's well aware of the risks—a misstep, a missed beat, harsh criticism, or even an injury. But she's equally aware of the rewards that await beyond those risks: the thunderous applause, the intoxicating personal satisfaction, those fleeting moments of sheer glory.

Every time she steps onto the stage, she dances with a delicate balance. Risks don't intimidate her; they ignite a fire within her. Even a stumble or a fall becomes an opportunity to rise, improve, and grow. This dance is her gateway to mastering her art and inching closer to her wildest dreams.

And let's not forget that rebellious high school student trying to figure out his college major—a decision that comes with a hefty dose of risks and rewards. Choosing a path driven by passion might risk financial stability, while opting for a lucrative field could jeopardize personal fulfillment. The student navigates the web of trade-offs, honing his mindful mastery. It's a bit of a head-scratcher, but it's through making this choice that he shapes his future, carving out his unique path.

And that's where self-reflection comes into play. The student gazes into his inner mirror, pondering his interests, strengths, and long-term aspirations. He might ask:

- Do I genuinely love what I'm considering doing?

- Am I ready to face the challenges it entails?

- What are the risks, and what are the rewards?

Through reflection, he navigates the dance of decision-making with a sharper sense of self-awareness and direction, sashaying toward his own truth.

The entrepreneurs might ask:

- Are we chasing a big win or setting ourselves up for a big fall?

- Are our choices opening doors to reward, or are we walking into a booby trap of risk?

- When it comes to our current path, is the finish line a victory stand or a steep cliff?

And the dancer might ask:

- Is the grindstone practice sharpening my skills or wearing me down before I reach peak performance?

- Is the applause at the end of a performance the sweet reward for hard work, or is it a deceptive lullaby encouraging complacency in my art?

- In my pursuit of sheer glory, am I refining my technique and resilience, or am I neglecting my physical and emotional well-being?

In each of these remarkable examples, the dance of mindful mastery takes center stage. It's a dance that demands our active participation amid the whirlwind of change, an embrace of risks that says, 'Bring it on!' and an unwavering pursuit of rewards that tantalize our souls. It's about understanding the stakes, making choices, learning from our epic faceplants, and continually evolving into the most awe-inspiring dancers of our own remarkable lives.

Embrace the risks worth taking with a resounding 'Yes!' and confidently reject anything that hinders your progress with a firm 'No!' Most importantly, keep evolving, reflecting, and becoming the skilled performers who captivate the audience on life's exhilarating stage.

Chapter Thirty-Two

Ripping off the Band-Aid

What Do I Have to Let Go Of?

"Some people believe holding on and hanging in there are signs of great strength. However, there are times when it takes much more strength to know when to let go and then do it."

— SYNDICATED COLUMNIST ANN LANDERS

Letting go? Isn't that just a fancy term for finally admitting that your closet full of 'skinny jeans from five years ago' will never see the light of day again? There are times when we might feel like we're hanging on the edge of a precipice, fingers raw and bleeding, muscles tensed like a cat ready to pounce on its prey. It's as if the whole world is conspiring against us, pushing us ever closer to the abyss.

In these moments, conventional wisdom tells us that strength means clinging on with all our might, refusing to let go, and holding on for dear life. But let's face it; if the strength to hold onto old junk in our garages equated to real power, we'd all be superheroes with a side gig in extreme weightlifting competitions. That's not quite how it works.

Yet the legendary columnist Ann Landers proposed a strikingly different interpretation of strength. She suggested that, paradoxically, true strength might lie not in tenacious endurance but in the act of letting go. And so, in Landers' spirit, we find ourselves probing a fundamentally transformative question: 'What do I have to let go of?'

It's as if she handed us a parachute and said, 'Jump!'. Now, I know what you're thinking: 'Is she seriously asking me to jump out of a perfectly good airplane?'

Well, metaphorically speaking, yes. We're not advocating for a spontaneous skydiving adventure, but rather an exploration of what we carry in our mental backpacks and whether some of that cargo is weighing us down unnecessarily.

Seriously now, in reading this, you might be thinking. 'Are you suggesting I just release all my responsibilities and float away on a cloud of carefree bliss?'.

Well… not exactly. We're not advocating for a complete abandonment of duties or a total disregard for reality. After all, bills still need to be paid, and deadlines won't magically disappear if we close our eyes and wish them away. But maybe, just maybe, there's a method to this madness.

The answer to the question about what to let go is as complex and unique as a snowflake or a fingerprint. For some, it may involve shedding toxic relationships or dead-end jobs. For others, it could mean surrendering worn-out beliefs or self-limiting perceptions that are as fashionable as last year's jeans. But the real challenge, and the real strength, lies not in pinpointing what needs to be released, but in actually setting it free.

In ancient Greek mythology, Atlas was condemned by Zeus to hold up the celestial heavens for eternity—a symbol of endurance against insurmountable weight. I don't know about you, but I can't imagine a gym routine that would prepare anyone for that kind of upper body workout. And yet, I can't help but wonder his true strength would have emerged had he chosen to let go, to refuse the imposed burden, to accept the unknown consequences. This idea contradicts our traditional understanding of power and resilience, inviting us to consider strength not as an act of resistance but one of surrender.

Let's bring this concept into our own messy lives. We've all been there, juggling an absurd number of responsibilities and tasks, thinking we're acrobats in a never-ending circus. We're convinced that doing it all is the ultimate badge of honor. But let's be real; no superhero cape can save us from the perils of an overflowing to-do list. It's time to put on our thinking caps instead.

Learning to triage tasks, we become like seasoned emergency responders in the face of a crisis. Just as a skilled first responder assesses the situation, prioritizes resources, and makes critical decisions, we too must evaluate the urgency and significance of our own tasks and commitments. It's akin to determining which emergencies require immediate attention and action, ensuring that the most critical, important issues are addressed first.

We create space for what genuinely matters when we acknowledge our limitations and surrender to the art of letting go. We can focus our energy and attention on the things that align with our values, spark joy, and contribute to our personal growth. This act of conscious triage empowers us to make intentional choices, set healthy boundaries, and liberate ourselves from the tyranny of trying to do it all.

It's at this point that we transition from ancient teachings to contemporary reality and my experience attending the TED Women conference. The vibrant energy is palpable from the moment you step into the registration room. And amid this buzzing atmosphere, an encounter occurred that epitomized the philosophy we've been exploring.

As I went through the registration process, a woman, who was representing the start-up The Giving Keys, approached me. She handed me a necklace adorned with an old-fashioned key, and on it was engraved the powerful phrase 'Letting go'. She explained that I should wear it, and when I encountered someone who could find value in its message, I should pass it on.

I loved this. With such amazing people attending the conference, I wondered who would benefit from the message on the necklace.

During the conference, one of the intriguing activities called Brain Dates caught my attention. As a Coach to the TED Fellows and Senior Fellows, I was invited to participate in this unique experience. The concept was simple: I had to go online and state what knowledge or expertise I could offer to those seeking advice, along with my availability. Once someone expressed interest in connecting with me and presented their specific request, I had the option to accept or decline the invitation.

Without wasting any time, someone reached out to me. Her self-introduction was nothing short of captivating. Not only did she mention that she was seeking a career transition due to burnout, but she also hinted at a multifaceted background involving aviation and mentorship. There was a complexity and depth in her words that promised an intriguing conversation, one that would surely be as enlightening for me as it would be for her. It was this multi-layered aspect of her persona that intrigued me, so I accepted her request and agreed to meet her at the designated time.

Our Brain Date was limited to half an hour, emphasizing efficiency and impact. Her request was to seek guidance on transitioning into a new career, as she was experiencing burnout and wanted to explore potential solutions.

As she began speaking, I was absolutely amazed. This extraordinary woman was on the verge of completing her master's degree, she was one of a handful of attendees training to become an astronaut, she was working as an Air Force Pilot (which was her day job), and additionally, she was mentoring a group of young women. She was deeply passionate about each aspect of her life, which posed a significant challenge. How could she identify anything to let go of?

Suddenly, I remembered the necklace, took it off, and handed it to her. It was a pay-it-forward moment. I encouraged her to wear the necklace as long as she needed to and then to pass it on to someone else who would benefit from the message.

In her case, her day job and completing her master's degree were non-negotiable, as was her commitment to astronaut training. This meant her mentoring position was the only area she could potentially adjust. However, she expressed reluctance to give it up entirely. But through our conversation, she realized that letting go didn't have to be permanent.

She could pause her mentoring responsibilities temporarily until a future time when she had more space in her life to take it up again. The mere act of having this conversation provided her with an immense sense of relief, as the overwhelming burden she carried began to dissolve.

Author Alan Watts puts it beautifully: "In the process of letting go, you will lose many things from the past, but you will find yourself."

When we're running in all directions and trying to manage multiple and sometimes conflicting priorities, there's no space or time to just be and settle into a rhythm of life. We're just too focused on getting from point A to point B.

Indeed, true strength is not found in clinging desperately to the familiar, but in having the guts to release that which is no longer beneficial or even relevant, to adapt, and to evolve. It's about mustering the courage to face the uncertainty that lies ahead, knowing that what once served us may now hinder our progress. Strength demands that we confront our fears head-on, not with blind stubbornness, but with vulnerable openness, acknowledging that life's beauty lies not in standing still, but in its ever-changing dance.

So, when faced with the question, 'What do I have to let go of?' we embark on a journey of self-discovery, a quest to uncover the essence of true strength, a bold exploration of life's infinite possibilities. What specific question can help to triage my thoughts, beliefs, and relationships to determine what is worth holding onto and what I should release?

- What are the core values and principles that reign supreme in my life, and how can I fearlessly judge my thoughts, beliefs, and relationships against them?

- Do my current thoughts, beliefs, and relationships align with the fierce persona I aspire to, or do they need a savage makeover?

- What recurring patterns or negative thoughts or beliefs keep crashing my party, and are they fueling my growth or holding me back?

- How do my relationships enrich my well-being, personal growth, and overall happiness? Are they awesome allies or toxic vampires?

- Which thoughts, beliefs, or relationships bring the thunder and ignite my soul, and which ones drain my energy and stunt my development? How do I separate the (s)heroes from the zeroes?

- Who dares to influence my thoughts, beliefs, and relationships? And do they align with my raw, authentic self or are they just posers in my parade?

- What fierce boundaries or criteria should I lay down to determine which relationships make the cut—that are nurturing, supportive, and aligned with my growth—and which ones need a stern eviction notice?

- Are my beliefs and thought patterns rooted in ancient history or unfounded nonsense? How can I boldly challenge and scrutinize their validity?

- What epic experiences or cold-hard facts should I gather to judge the effectiveness and relevance of my current beliefs and thought patterns? (And show me the receipts.)

- Bottom line: how might I consistently size up my thoughts, beliefs, and relationships to ensure they march in line with an ever-evolving sense of self and purpose?

Letting go isn't an act of defeat—it is an emancipation. It's a process of shedding, a courageous embrace of vulnerability, a daring leap of faith into the realm of the unknown. In surrendering, we unearth our true strength—not in stubborn resistance to what is, but in the audacious acceptance of what could be.

Those pivotal moments—when we come face to face with significant life events or profound realizations that make it clear our life will never be the same—these are the moments when the question 'What do I have to let go of?' becomes paramount. These critical junctures serve as turning points that demand a reevaluation of priorities and compel us to release anything that no longer serves our well-being.

Whether it's a soulless job, a toxic relationship, responsibilities competing for your attention, or a belief system that has lost its resonance, these moments push us to embrace change and dive into the unknown.

By releasing the past and stepping into the future fearlessly, we emerge stronger, wiser, and more resilient than ever before.

Chapter Thirty-Three

Pivotal Moments

"There are moments which mark your life, moments when you realize nothing will ever be the same and time is divided into two parts: before this and after this."

— FROM THE MOVIE FALLEN, WARNER BROS, 1998

The universe is the ultimate comedian, and let's face it, sometimes we're the punchline. It manipulates the course of existence like a skilled strategist, introducing unforeseen twists into our carefully drafted narratives with the precision of a seasoned prankster. It's the universe's equivalent of a pie in the face, unexpected, messy, and a brutal assault to one's pride. These rippling peaks and valleys are the pivotal moments that punctuate our lives, slicing time into a jigsaw of 'befores' and 'afters'.

Consider this: one moment, we're the authors of our stories, blissfully penning our future on the blank pages of tomorrow. We have planned our plotline meticulously and orchestrated our characters diligently. And then? Our own narrative rebels against us. It devours our expectations, then burps out startling alternatives, spinning us in a new direction faster than a comet on a collision course. The before is wiped out. The after is yet to be filled. We're left in the indeterminate, unsettling now, suspended in a limbo of could-have-beens and what-nows.

Remember what the character John Hobbes in the movie *Fallen* said at the start of this chapter? Moments like these slice our lives into 'before' and 'after'. These are the points where life's linear path morphs into a kaleidoscopic tapestry—dazzling, intricate, yet inexplicably beautiful. It's akin to watching a thrilling movie or reading an engaging novel where the plot twists make us gasp, recoil, weep, or laugh. They introduce the conflict; the spice that makes the narrative memorable.

So, here's the deal: these curveballs are actually our chance to show what we're made of. Cool, right? We can either crumble under the weight of the unforeseen or rise from the ashes, reborn. Remember, it's not the plot twist that defines our story, but how we choose to write the ensuing chapters. Do we let our story end on a cliffhanger, forever teetering on the edge of uncertainty, or do we seize our pen back from the universe and craft a powerful resolution?

Here's the idea: when life decides to surprise you with a curveball, don't duck—swing! Sure, it's unsettling when plans go haywire, but that's also when life hands you a clean slate and a new field of possibilities. This is your cue to show some grit and stage your epic comeback.

You see, when our plans go off the rails, that's our real moment to shine. We get to show off our mad skills at navigating life's challenges—doing it all with style, courage, and a sprinkle of sass.

These moments come in all shapes and sizes. They might shatter like a victorious glass ceiling or sneak up like a melancholic melody playing softly in the background. A tragic accident, the loss of a loved one, an illness, tornado, a sudden career breakthrough, an unexpected relocation—each one leaves an indelible mark on the pages of one's personal history.

Every now and then, life throws us into a wild whirlwind of change. We cling desperately to the familiar, the comfortable; but life, in all its infinite wisdom, chuckles and says, 'Nope! I've got other plans for you'. We find ourselves floundering in uncertainty, in the eerie calm at the center of the storm. Yet, in the middle of this chaos, an opportunity emerges, an invitation to redefine ourselves, to reinvent our very essence, and to truly grasp the indomitable spirit of human resilience.

These big moments? They're not just about what happens to us, but how we deal. It's like being handed the steering wheel in a storm. It's human to fear change, but embracing it, seeing it as a wise old teacher of the soul, is the mark of true wisdom. Our reactions to these pivotal moments give them the weight that they will carry in our hearts.

Even the brainiacs can't agree—some call these moments crises, while others say they're transitions. But no matter the label, they recognize that turning points possess an inherent power, a raw potential to reshape the course of our lives.

When we find ourselves teetering on the edge of uncertainty—peering into the vast canyon of the unknown—do we falter, do we retreat, or do we take a daring leap, trusting that the safety net will magically appear?

In these moments, it's crucial to remember the power we hold.

Picture this: I'm at the airport, ready to embark on an ungodly-early flight. Knowing full well the security and customs hoops I need to jump through, I arrive 90 minutes ahead of schedule, determined not to miss my flight. Can't risk any airport adventures, now, can we? And Nexus was supposed to make clearing customs a breeze.

Or so I thought.

After going through security, I made my way to the Nexus line, which is a border pass for expedited crossing over the Canadian and United States Borders. To my surprise, one of the young border officers whom I had coached in the past was staffing another kiosk, giving me a friendly wave. Being the first one in line since the office opened, he looked at my documentation, glanced at me, and said: "This is your lucky day!"

"Oh, really? In what way is it lucky?" I responded, intrigued.

"Absolutely. As a way keeping people in the program 'honest', we have a little lottery where we randomly select someone for secondary inspection. Congratulations, you're the lucky winner!"

He then directed me to where I needed to go.

Curiosity piqued, I walked into the back room, eager to see what this hidden world held. Watching others being put through the wringer for smuggling contraband or failing to declare items was oddly fascinating. In the midst of my observation, the same young customs agent I had worked with entered the room and walked casually into an open office, waving at me as he passed by.

Apparently, he mentioned to his supervisor: "Oh, is Donna coaching you, too?"

His supervisor, clearly perplexed, asked him to explain.

The agent simply responded: "It's better if you ask her directly."

With that, he left the office and returned to the main Customs area.

Finally, it was my turn to enter that same open office. The supervising officer asked me about my destination and the purpose of my trip. I responded concisely, receiving a nod. Then came the question of what I did for a living.

I decided to take a different approach and said: "If it's alright with you, I'd prefer to show you rather than tell you. I promise there's no hidden agenda. It's just much easier to demonstrate and then explain why and how I do what I do once you've experienced a bit of it."

He agreed, and so our conversation began. Starting off with asking about his tenure as a border officer, I inquired: "How long have you been a border officer?"

"Sixteen years," he replied.

"Has your role changed for you over those 16 years?" I asked, curious to understand his perspective.

"I've had two promotions during that time," he answered.

"Any pivotal moments along the way?" I probed further.

"Definitely," he replied without hesitation.

"What was the most impactful pivotal moment for you?" I asked, wanting to delve deeper into his personal experience to build a connection.

"9/11," he responded solemnly. "That changed everything. I haven't been able to sleep well since then, constantly reviewing the people I let into the country, always wondering if I might have inadvertently allowed a terrorist in."

I paused, giving him a moment to absorb what he had just revealed.

Then, I said: "That's where my work begins. That pivotal moment redefined your work, how you make decisions, and how your fears might influence those decisions. It's about processing all of that, becoming so self-aware that these thoughts and fears no longer dictate our choices. Instead, they inform them or serve as a reality check, helping us do the best we can with the information and resources available."

He immediately asked: "How much time do we have?"

It was 5:45am, I had a flight to catch at 6:30am (and I hadn't even had my coffee yet). I shared that with him. He assured me that he would make sure I caught my flight, promised to fetch me a cup of coffee, and arranged for someone else to take over his duties while we talked for half an hour.

After our conversation, he expressed amazement at how recognizing that pivotal moment in relation to himself and his work had become a pivotal moment in its own right. He assured me that he would never forget our conversation and how it had shifted his thinking.

Such pivotal moments—unexpected and disruptive—force us to confront difficult realities and can take various forms, such as a health diagnosis, the loss of a loved one, or a major life change. Yet, they all share a common thread: they compel us to respond. These profound divisions of time are integral to the human experience.

I often find myself delineating my life based on moments like before or after cancer, or before or after the tornado struck. Each of these pivotal moments is as unique as every breath we take, an exploration from the realm of 'before' to the domain of 'after'. These moments are not just tick marks on a calendar, but the incisions where the scalpel of destiny has left its mark.

Life, the masterful shapeshifter, also takes delight in reshaping our well-laid plans, and catching us unawares with the thrill of transformation. But these pivotal moments are not mere roadblocks; they are invitations to stretching and to growth, to acquiring wisdom, and to redefining our existence. Like artists, these moments sculpt the marble of our lives, paint the master strokes of our unique journey. These are the instances that lay bare the immensity of our strength and the indomitable spirit within.

Whether you call them milestones or game-changers, think of them as life's earthquakes—shaking up everything you thought you knew. They disrupt our monotonous routine, forcing us to rebuild, reimagine, and redefine who we are and what our lives mean. This is a wild ride. It is not a steady stream, but a series of spasmodic leaps, jolting us between 'before' and 'after'.

It's as though our existence is pieced together from a patchwork quilt of disparate moments, each fragment bursting with its distinctive texture, hue, and emotional resonance. Before and after—what? Love? Loss? Joy? Betrayal?

From the minor ripples to the cataclysmic temblors, these moments mold our sense of self and our understanding of the world. They are as unique as every breath we take, and yet, they are a universal human experience.

So, how might you identify your 'before' and 'after'? How do you delve into this intricate web of memories and moments? Take a moment to pause. Close your eyes and rewind the film of your life. Search for those moments of profound change when you can clearly say: 'I was one person before this moment, and someone entirely different after.'

They might be traumatic, like a natural disaster or illness. They might be euphoric, like falling in love or the birth of a child. Or they might be mundane, yet equally transformative: an inspiring book, a chance encounter, or a sudden realization while staring at the stars.

And what do you do when you find them? First, acknowledge their power. The 'afters' aren't always easy. They can be raw, uncomfortable, even painful. But they are the points at which you've grown, changed, evolved. Next, embrace them. Lean into the discomfort, the uncertainty, the thrill. In these seismic shifts you'll find resilience, a capacity for joy, and an ability to adapt and thrive.

So, there you have it. Life's all about those 'whoa' moments, right? One minute you're going down a familiar path, and the next, bam! You're looking at things in a whole new light. And honestly, that's pretty awesome. These curveballs, challenges, or whatever you want to call them—they don't just shake things up; they make us who we are.

Don't get me wrong; it's not always a walk in the park. But think about it: Would you really want to just breeze through life without a scratch? Probably not. It's the tricky bits that make the good parts even better.

The thing to remember is, these moments aren't just random interruptions to our regularly scheduled programming. They're chances for us to grow, to learn, and to get a better grip on what makes us tick. So, the next time you find yourself at one of life's crossroads, take a beat. Take it all in and remember that you've got the power to turn that moment into something really special.

And hey, while you're at it, keep an eye out for the little things, too. Sometimes the smallest changes can make the biggest impact, and that's worth keeping in mind as we navigate this crazy rollercoaster called life.

Chapter Thirty-Four

Noticing the Not-So-Obvious

The Art of Perception and Possibility

"One of the best things that you can do for yourself is to consciously notice the things you don't usually notice. It is a sign of great deep awareness to see what was obvious but was never noticed before."

— INDIAN AMERICAN AUTHOR DEEPAK CHOPRA

We're all in a perpetual game of hide and seek with reality. Peek-a-boo, says the universe, as it flashes its marvelous secrets in front of our eyes, and then cleverly tucks them behind a curtain of the mundane. Each day, we unwrap ourselves from the cocoons of sleep and dive into our own peculiar Groundhog Day, replete with predictably caffeinated neighbors drawing our attention. Life, at first glance, might seem as consistent as a stubborn pudding refusing to budge from the bowl.

Bundled up in our little cocoons of 'routine', when every day is a merry dance of habitual meanderings, we wake up, rush through breakfast, and jump onto the treadmill of life. Look, there's Mrs. Adams, who offers her daily morning wave with her dog, a whirlwind of wagging tail and boundless enthusiasm. And here's your dependable coffee, with its comforting promise to fortify you for the day's challenges. You might believe life is as predictable as a morning traffic jam, unmoving and unyielding.

But wait! Has Mrs. Adams always had that interesting hat? Was that dimple in your partner's cheek always this adorable? The world is packed to the brim with exquisite details that we're just too busy, too tired, too disconnected, or perhaps too lazy to see.

Like a mischievous street magician performing an incessant sleight of hand, the universe uses its trusty top hat. The trick? To make the obvious appear not so obvious. But here's where we're mistaken: the magic doesn't lie in the trick; it lies in the reveal. The awe. The wide-eyed surprise. The chills down your spine when you see what was always there but was somehow invisible.

Just imagine if we took the time to observe—to really see. Not just the morning sun rising, but the way it coyly peeks from behind the curtain of the horizon, as if unsure of its brilliance. Not just the coffee, but the artful ballet of steam rising from the cup, carrying the aroma that holds promises of future ideas and inspiration. Not just the people with whom we cross paths, but their laugh lines, their stories, their silent struggles and victories, all echoed in their eyes.

Albert Einstein famously said: "There are only two ways to live your life. One is as though nothing is a miracle. The other is as though everything is a miracle."

So, why choose the former when the latter offers such wonders?

Now, imagine yourself at the starting line, toeing the edge of your comfort zone with the world of possibility spread out before you. It's an exciting and yet, admittedly, terrifying vista, crammed with unknowns and uncertainties. But hasn't the practice of noticing taught us to embrace the unknown, to find beauty in the details, and to relish the mystery?

Stepping into the pursuit of dreams is much like stepping into a darkened room. At first, we may hesitate, unsure of what lies within. But as we take those first few brave steps, we find our eyes adjusting to the darkness, revealing shapes and contours previously unseen. The unknown becomes known, the mystery a beautiful enigma to be unraveled.

Unleash the child within—the one who points at the sky in wonder and sees shapes in the clouds, who finds fairy worlds in dew drops and laughs at their own echoes. This is not an invitation to abandon reality, rather an urge to embrace a broader, more colorful one. It's an art, the art of perception and possibility.

'But wait,' you might object. 'What about the bills to be paid, the work to be finished, the deadlines to be met?'

Yes, the responsibilities of adult life are real and overwhelming. However, let's rethink them. Those bills are a testament to the shelter over your head, the warmth of your home, the food on your plate. That work is a manifestation of your skills and capabilities, an acknowledgment of your contribution to society. Those deadlines? They are milestones marking your progress, your growth, your evolution. Through the lens of perception and possibility, even mundane obligations can unfurl to reveal hidden wonders.

Perhaps you're saying, 'I've tried, but it's just not possible for me'. Well, possibility is not a given, it's an art. Like any other art, it demands practice, patience, and a hefty dose of curiosity. Just as an artist sees a blank canvas as a realm of endless potential, each day, each moment, can be your canvas. Can you draw a world that surprises and delights?

Look around, and you'll discover that we're bound by the invisible threads of interconnectedness. The same energy that fuels the sun is mirrored in the flicker of an idea in your brain, the rhythmic pounding of your heart. Even in our most disconnected moments, we're intrinsically connected to the grand cosmic dance. We are stardust come alive, after all.

Imagine if we used this awareness to influence our interactions with others. What if we saw beyond the exterior of the grumpy shopkeeper or the silent coworker? Behind every furrowed brow, every hardened exterior, lie stories waiting to be heard, souls yearning to connect. By opening ourselves to others' experiences, we can foster empathy and understanding, weaving a more compassionate and inclusive social fabric.

The act of noticing is akin to a domino effect. Once you start, you find it cascading through all aspects of your life, propelling you towards a richer, more profound understanding of your existence. This begs the question: what is stopping you? Fear, perhaps? The fear of upheaval, of facing the unfamiliar? Remember, though, fear is but a signal, a signpost in a journey towards growth. In the face of fear, recall the magic of the street magician; the trick is not to avoid, but to reveal, to marvel. Behind the curtain of fear lies a realm filled with breathtaking spectacles.

In the cosmic scheme of things, our lives are but fleeting moments, a blink of the eye of eternity. As we hurtle through time and space on this pale blue dot, what could be more empowering than to embrace each moment with an open heart, a keen eye, and a relentless curiosity? It's time to turn the 'not-so-obvious' into 'oh-so-miraculous'. Dive into the ocean of perception and possibility. Who knows what treasures you'll find?

This is the art of noticing, the art of transforming the ordinary into the extraordinary. It is in this alchemical process where we truly begin to live, to connect, and to celebrate the grandeur of existence. In each moment lies a universe of possibility. It's time we opened our eyes to see it.

Are we overlooking what is right in front of us? The answer becomes evident when the world turns into a blur of 'sameness', the details fade into obscurity, and our senses grow numb to the symphony of life unfolding around us. Consider this:

1. **Perception: a prison or a playground?** Perception is a mighty tool that paints reality. Are you using it to build walls or crafting a sprawling playground teeming with opportunities? The way we perceive the world is not a life sentence. It's a starting point for infinite possibilities.

2. **Routine or rut?** The daily grind can feel as unyielding as steel bars. Yet, within this perceived confinement lies an invitation to play, to find novelty in the monotonous. Can you perceive the cadence in the chaos, the pattern in the random, the poetry in the mundane? What if our daily routines were instead an unchartered path to discovery, a breadcrumb trail to the unexpected?

3. **Comfort zone or danger zone?** The bubble of comfort can be enticing, lulling us into complacency. But when does comfort become discomfort? When does familiarity become monotony? Reflect: could your safe haven be a breeding ground for stagnation? Might the danger lie not in venturing out but in remaining cocooned?

4. **Sensory deprivation or sensory exploration?** We often retreat into the digital world, where we are bombarded with a cacophony of sounds and images from screens. What if we hit pause and let our senses roam in the tangible world? Can you hear the symphony in the silence, taste the story in your food, feel history beneath your fingertips? Consider a digital detox, not as a punishment, but as an exploration of sensory bliss.

5. **Unnoticed or undiscovered?** What is it that you're not seeing in your day-to-day life? The barista's shy smile? The elderly man's wise eyes? The gentle curve of the trees against the sky? Think about it: could the unnoticed be an undiscovered treasure chest, waiting for us to break open its lock with the key to attention?

6. **Living or existing?** Each day we wake, we eat, we work, and we sleep. But is that living or merely existing? Could we be mistaking the ebb and flow of survival for truly embracing life? Dare to ask: what

would life look like if every moment, every breath, every heartbeat was an opportunity for magic, a passport to the extraordinary?

7. **Mind-full or mindful?** Do you often find your mind full of anxieties, racing towards an uncertain future or anchored in a past that no longer exists? What if you chose to be mindful instead, wholly immersed in the present? Imagine if every moment were a dance, with you, its enthralled dancer, lost in the rhythm, entranced by the melody, and alive to the beat.

Wear your spectacles of curiosity and dive headfirst into the ocean of hidden treasures because the world is chock-full of details just waiting to be discovered. Take that leap. Notice the not-so-obvious. And who knows? You might just stumble upon a universe within a grain of sand.

Chapter Thirty-Five

Tuning Out the Noise

Listening to Your Inner Voice

"The most powerful force on earth is the human soul on fire. Tune out the noise and ignite yours."

— SOLDIER AND WRITER FERDINAND FOCH

Throughout this book, we've explored the contours of life with levity and wit, punctuating our journey with a bit of laughter. These, after all, are the seasonings that make the dish of life more palatable, turning the ordinary into the extraordinary and adding a silver lining to the darkest clouds.

Have you ever felt overwhelmed by the noise around you?

Yet, humor is not just a tool to draw smiles or elicit chuckles—it's a mirror that reflects our deepest truths, an ally in our quest for self-discovery. As we near the end of our journey, I invite you to embrace a shift in tone, to slip into a more introspective mood; to set aside, just for a moment, the enticing allure of humor, and focus instead on the serious, significant, soulful side of our journey.

This chapter is not about wit or wisecrack, but about wisdom. It's not about the clamor, but about quiet introspection. It's not about listening to the noise, but about tuning it out. It's about hearing our inner voice, the authentic self that often gets drowned in the relentless roar of life. It's a call to turn inward, to pause, and listen, truly listen, to the voice within. The voice that has been with us since our first breath, whispering insights, singing songs of intuition, and holding a mirror to our deepest, most authentic selves. It's a voice that doesn't demand attention, but commands it, a voice that's heard not with the ears but with the heart.

In this digital era, where tweets chirp, posts reverberate, and stories can vanish even before imprinting on our collective consciousness, it's a challenge to hear your inner voice amidst the turmoil. How much time do you spend on social media daily? Do you feel it enriches your life or takes away from it? Overwhelmed by a cascade of voices, we've unknowingly auctioned our most precious asset—our very own voice—in exchange for retweets and likes. And yet, it's not the clamor but the whisper that holds true power; the subtle hum of our own spirit is what houses the profound truths about who we are and what we aspire to be.

We can take inspiration from well-known figures who have managed to do this successfully. Consider the actor Jim Carrey. At the height of his fame and fortune, Carrey took a hiatus from his career. Have you ever felt the need to retreat and reconnect with your own self? What stopped you? He was struggling with depression and the pressures of Hollywood, his life filled with the din of fame and expectation. He chose to tune out that noise, turning to spirituality, painting, and meditation to reconnect with his authentic self. Carrey's journey is a testament to the power of listening to our inner voice, even when external success seems to drown it out.

As Ferdinand Foch once aptly observed: "The most powerful force on earth is the human soul on fire." But what does it mean to have the soul on fire? What sets your soul on fire? When was the last time you felt truly passionate about something? It's the awakened spirit, the animated self. It's the indomitable force that sparks genius, fuels passion, and births revolutions.

The soul ablaze is the touchstone of living with intention, steering life not as a ship adrift on the currents of circumstance but as a vessel propelled by a wind of one's own making. It is to live authentically, to honor the singular cadence of our spirits, embodying power as a profound and intimate mastery of self. To tune out the noise is an act of radical self-care, a decision to curate one's auditory environment and choose silence over sound, stillness over motion.

Arianna Huffington, the co-founder of the *Huffington Post*, provides a shining example of this principle. Have you ever experienced a wake-up call that made you reevaluate your priorities? When she collapsed from exhaustion, Huffington reevaluated her approach to success. She started to listen more closely to her inner voice, which guided her towards a more balanced life. She later founded Thrive Global, a company dedicated to promoting well-being and productivity, clearly illustrating the transformative power of tuning out the external noise and listening to our internal needs.

It is about discerning which voices, noises, and influences serve our growth and well-being and which ones merely stoke the flames of anxiety, self-doubt, and confusion. Are there voices or influences in your life that you feel are toxic or unhelpful? How could you minimize their impact? Listening to our inner voice is an act of understanding and nurturing, honoring our unique essence, and dancing to the rhythm that resonates with the deepest reaches of our being. Tuning out the noise is not about isolating oneself, but fostering an internal symphony, a harmonious interplay between silence and the soul's voice. Our actions then reflect our authentic selves, the music of our inner voice, and we cease to exist merely in reaction to the world around us, instead, beginning to shape our reality.

The soul on fire becomes a beacon of potential, a testament to the latent power within us all. This is where we engage with introspection, grapple with the questions that not only ignite our souls but fan their flames into a roaring, transformative blaze. It's not about seeking immediate answers, but about exploring and examining, opening doors within us rather than closing them with definitive responses.

Who are you when no one is watching? What ignites your passion, quickens your heartbeat, and sparks a light in your eyes? Living in these questions allows us to remain open to what isn't evident, to the secrets that the soul has yet to reveal, and to the pathways yet to be discovered. As we engage in this dialogue with ourselves, we create an environment for our power to unfold, propelling us towards our most heartfelt ambitions and dreams.

Where do you begin?

First, become aware of the noise that surrounds you. It may be the relentless stream of social media updates, the constant bombardment of news, or the cacophony of other people's opinions. Recognize that not all voices are deserving of our attention and energy. Selectively filter out the distractions that hinder the ability to listen to your inner voice.

Next, find solace in solitude. Create moments of silence in the day, away from the relentless buzz of technology and the demands of the external world. In these quiet spaces, you can cultivate a deeper connection with yourself, allowing your inner voice to rise to the surface. Practice mindfulness and introspection. Engage in activities that foster self-reflection, such as journaling, meditation, or taking solitary walks in nature. These practices help us tune in to our inner voice, to hear its whispers and wisdom amidst the noise.

Surround yourself with uplifting influences. Seek out individuals who inspire and support the journey of self-discovery. Engage in meaningful conversations that encourage deep introspection and growth. Limit exposure to toxic relationships and negative environments that dampen the spirit.

Embrace the power of boundaries. Set limits on the amount of external noise that infiltrates our lives. Create sacred spaces and times for introspection, free from the distractions of technology and the demands of others. Do you currently have a 'sacred space' for yourself? What does it look like? Respect your own needs and prioritize well-being.

Finally, trust your intuition. Cultivate a sense of trust in the inner voice. Recognize that we possess a wealth of wisdom within, waiting to guide us on our path. When was the last time you truly trusted your intuition, and what was the outcome?

Satya Nadella, the CEO of Microsoft, demonstrated the power of trusting his own intuition. Upon assuming leadership, he prioritized a cultural shift within the company, recognizing the importance of empathy from his personal life, which ran contrary to the prevailing ethos in the tech industry. His trust in his inner voice transformed Microsoft into a more collaborative, innovative, and successful entity.

Tune in to your instincts, honor your gut feelings, and have the courage to follow the whispers of your soul. By actively tuning out the noise, we create a sanctuary for our inner voice to be heard. We reclaim our power, align with our authentic selves, and live life on our own terms. It is a journey of self-discovery, transformation, and growth, a journey fueled by our inner voice and ignited soul.

So, let us tune out the noise, listen to our inner voices, and open ourselves to a life lived to the fullest.

Epilogue

"Change and growth take place when a person has risked himself and dares to become involved with experimenting with his own life."

— PSYCHOLOGIST AND AUTHOR HERBERT OTTO

That profound quote from psychologist and author Herbert Otto is just as true today as when it was first articulated. And speaking of timeless wisdom, let's not forget what author and professor John A. Shedd succinctly captured with his words: "A ship in harbor is safe, but that is not what ships are built for."

So, if we connect the dots between these two gems, what's the big message here? It's pretty simple, really. Hanging out in your comfort zone feels good and safe, but that's not what we're here for. Just like those ships are meant for the open sea, we're wired for curiosity, self-discovery, and leveling up in life.

Our tales? Nah, they're not about playing it safe. They're penned in the wild and the unpredictable. Every question, every choice, and every little brave move is us setting our course, getting ready for some serious wind in our sails.

Change is like that morning coffee—a kickstart. And growth? That's the extra shot of espresso. Sure, there might be some stormy seas ahead, but remember, countless individuals have navigated these waters before, and their stories can serve as beacons for your own journey.

As we near the end of this book, consider it not a conclusion but an initiation—a calling to move beyond what's familiar and comfortable. It's an invitation to navigate your life toward greater vistas of self-understanding and opportunity.

Allow your intuition to be your compass, steering you toward your most authentic self. While the path may be uncertain, it is within that very uncertainty that we find room for growth, learning, and insight.

As you prepare to set sail on your next chapter, let the lessons from these pages be your guide. Tune out the distractions and tune in to your own wisdom. The world is filled with hidden gems waiting to be discovered.

And so, I leave you not with a goodbye, but with a sense of expectancy for the adventures that await. Your sails are set, your compass aligned; now, all that remains is to chart your course toward the unknown. Here's to writing your next chapter with courage, curiosity, and unwavering commitment.

Bon voyage.

Questions We Pondered

What is the question I need to ask myself right now?

What is really happening here?

What do I really want to have happen?

What desired end result do I crave, and what am I willing to risk getting there?

What truly matters?

Who am I?

Who do I appear to be to others?

How do I show up?

Am I behaving in a way that aligns with the person I aspire to be?

Does my behavior reflect the qualities and character traits I admire and want to embody?

Am I living my life based on my true self or conforming to others' expectations?

What is triggering these emotions? What thoughts or external events led to these feelings?

What are my intuitive impulses? What actions or behaviors do I feel drawn to in this moment?

What are the consequences of the actions I feel drawn to take?

What assumptions or beliefs am I holding onto that are impacting my perception of this situation? What if I challenged these assumptions and looked at the situation from a different perspective?

What's really going on here?

Am I listening from a place of grace and gratitude or of judgment?

What am I supposed to learn from this?

Am I reacting from a place of fear or openness?

If I don't change, what will it cost me in the long run?

What do I need right now?

Is what I'm doing now something my future self will thank me for?

What about this is so perfect about this when it clearly isn't?

About the Author

Donna Karlin is a force of nature, a trailblazer, and a visionary in the realm of executive coaching, organizational psychology, organizational behavior, and leadership development. Donna has honed her expertise in working with executives, entrepreneurs, and high-potential leaders across diverse industries, including technology, healthcare, and entertainment. Her innate ability to unravel complex organizational dynamics and identify the root causes of individual and team challenges has made her a sought-after advisor for both Fortune 500 companies and startups alike.

Donna's coaching philosophy is rooted in her deep understanding of human behavior and her unwavering belief in the transformative power of conversation. She combines her sharp intellect, razor-sharp intuition, and empathetic nature to guide her clients towards breakthrough insights and profound personal growth.

Donna is also a captivating speaker, author, and thought leader. She has graced prestigious stages worldwide, including Actually She Can @TED Women, Innovations and Developments in the World of Trauma CIMA, HOW Mind Your Own Business, and IEEE, sharing her wisdom and inspiring audiences with her compelling stories and practical strategies for success.

As the founder of the Shadow Coaching® methodology, she has pioneered a groundbreaking approach that helps individuals explore the hidden aspects of their personalities and confront their inner obstacles. This unique framework has transformed countless lives, enabling individuals to unleash their full potential and achieve remarkable personal and professional breakthroughs.

Donna's impact on the coaching profession is immeasurable. As a Coach to TED Fellows and Senior Fellows, she leverages her expertise and guidance to contribute to the growth and development of individuals committed to global change. Additionally, as a Founding Fellow at the Harvard Institute of Coaching, McLean Medical School, she continues to shape the coaching landscape through her involvement in pioneering research and education.

Web: www.donnakarlin.com

https://noceilingjustskyinstitute.com/

LI: https://www.linkedin.com/in/donnakarlin/

Citation Station

Where Words Find Their Place

Preface

Rothfuss, Patrick. "It's the questions we can't answer that teach us the most. They teach us how to think. If you give a man an answer, all he gains is a little fact. But give him a question and he'll look for his own answers." *The Name of the Wind* (2007).

Wiesel, Elie. "In the word question, there is a beautiful word: quest. I love that word!" In an interview with Oprah Winfrey (2006).

Part One

Jung, Carl. "The most terrifying thing is to accept oneself completely."
https://excellencereporter.com/2020/01/06/carl-jung-on-the-wisdom-and-the-meaning-of-life/

Oldster, Kilroy J. "Self-transformation commences with a period of self-questioning. Questions lead to more questions, bewilderment leads to new discoveries, and growing personal awareness leads to transformation in how a person lives." *Dead Toad Scrolls* (2016)

Ferris, Karen. "Resilience is not just about bouncing back; it's about bouncing forward."LinkedIn post (June, 2019)

Carroll, Lewis. "Who in the world am I? Ah, that's the great puzzle." *Alice in Wonderland* (1865)

Whitman, Walt. "We are not one, but multitudes," Poem, *Leaves of Grass* (1855)

Liccione, Anthony. 'It's not about what you have on the outside that glitters in light, it's about what you have on the inside that shines in the dark.' https://www.goodreads.com/quotes/903947-it-s-not-what-you-have-on-the-outside-that-glitters

Waitley, Denis. "It is not what you are that holds you back, it's what you think you are not." —*The Psychology of Winning: Ten Qualities of a Total Winner* (1979)

Whyte, David. "The greatest tragedy is to live out someone else's life thinking it was your own." *The Sea in You Twenty Poems of Requited and Unrequited Love* (2016)

Ruiz, Don Miguel. "You are a unique and unrepeatable miracle of being. No one can be like you, and no one can ever take your place in the universe." *The Voice of Knowledge: A Practical Guide to Inner Peace* (2004)

Kent, Germany. "The way you show up in life will determine your success. Show up with passion, purpose, and positivity and you will be headed in the right direction" *The Hope Handbook: The Search for Personal Growth* (2015)

Cooley, Charles. "I'm not what I think I am, and I'm not what you think I am. I am what I think you think I am." *Human Nature and the Social Order: The Interplay of Man's Behaviors, Character and Personal Traits with His Society* (2018)

Bennett, Roy. "Be strong enough to stand up for yourself, be yourself, and speak your truth." *The Light in the Heart: Inspirational Thoughts for Living Your Best Life* (2021)

Baer, Jay. "The value of a question isn't in the answer. It's in the exploration of the idea, the conversation that the question provokes and the journey that you go on to get to an answer." *Talk Triggers: The Complete Guide to Creating Customers with Word of Mouth* (2018)

Culea, Nataşa Alina. "With a step forward and one backward, always between yesterday and tomorrow, we live in a question without answer: does the night end or the morning begin? And if it is a day when we can change everything, why don't we see it, although our eyes are wide open?" *Arlechinul: Povestea nespusă a Arlechinului* (translated to English as *The Harlequin: The Untold Story of the Harlequin*) (2020)

Fowles, John. "The most important questions in life can never be answered by anyone except oneself." *The Magus* (2001)

Part Two

Rim, J.R. "It's not about making the right choice. It's about making a choice and making it right." *Better to be Able to Love Than to be Loveable* (2015)

Robbins, Mel. "Asking yourself the right questions is like having a flashlight in the dark, illuminating the path ahead." The Mel Robbins Show

Obama, Michelle. "Let's invite one another in. Maybe then we can begin to fear less, to make fewer wrong assumptions, to let go of the biases and stereotypes that unnecessarily divide us." *Becoming* (2018)

Obama, Michelle. "There's power in allowing yourself to be known and heard, in owning your unique story, in using your authentic voice. And there's grace in being willing to know and hear others. This, for me, is how we become." *Becoming* (2018)

Yogev, Tomer. "A great relationship is about two things: first, appreciating the similarities, and second, respecting the differences." Interview with *Principal Post* (2022)

Tsu, Lao. "If you understand others, you are smart. If you understand yourself, you are illuminated. If you overcome others, you are powerful. If you overcome yourself, you have strength." *Tao Te Ching* (2022)

Ueland, Brenda. "Listening is a magnetic and strange thing, a creative force. The friends who listen to us are the ones we move toward. When we are listened to, it creates us, makes us unfold and expand." *If You Want to Write* (2019)

Salmansohn, Karen. "We cannot solve our problems alone; we need the help and wisdom of others" *Think Happy: Instant Peptalks to Boost Positivity* (2016)

Godin, Seth. "Taking a risk doesn't mean you'll always win, but it does mean you'll always learn something valuable." *The Dip: A Little Book That Teaches You When to Quit (and When to Stick)* (2007)

Galef, Julia. "The biggest obstacle to clarity is believing we already have it." *The Scout Mindset: Why Some People See Things Clearly and Others Don't* (2021)

Hill, Napoleon. "Desire is the starting point of all achievement, not a hope, not a wish, but a keen pulsating desire which transcends everything." *Think and Grow Rich* (1937)

Gordon, Graham. "Decision is a sharp knife that cuts clean and straight; indecision, a dull one that hacks and tears and leaves ragged edges behind it." Goodreads Post (https://www.goodreads.com/quotes/989825-decision-is-a-sharp-knife-that-cuts-clean-and-straight)

Mariboli, Steve. "The universe doesn't give you what you ask for with your thoughts; it gives you what you demand with your actions." *Unapologetically You: Reflections on Life and the Human Experience* (2013)

Fitzgerald, F. Scott. "The test of a first-rate intelligence is the ability to hold two opposed ideas in the mind at the same time, and still retain the ability to function." *The Crack-Up* (1936)

Part Three

Brown, Brené. "Fitting in and belonging are two separate things. Fitting in involves people changing themselves in order to be accepted. Belonging allows people to be accepted as they are." *The Gifts of Imperfection* (2010)

De Grey, Aubrey. "Your future self is watching you right now through memories." Goodreads Quote (https://www.goodreads.com/quotes/7791670-your-future-self-is-watching-you-right-now-through-your)

Bartlett, Steven. "Time is both free and priceless. The person you are now is a consequence of how you used your time in the past. The person you'll become in the future is a consequence of how you use your time in the present. Spend your time wisely, gamble it intrinsically and save it diligently." *Happy Sexy Millionaire: Unexpected Truths about Fulfilment, Love and Success* (2021)

Gaiman, Neil. "People think dreams aren't real just because they aren't made of matter, of particles. Dreams are real. But they are made of viewpoints, of images, of memories and puns and lost hopes." *The Sandman: Preludes and Nocturnes* (1988)

Karlin, Donna. "Sometimes we create our own traps. We build luxurious mink holes of comfort, only to realize that they are cages." *School of Shadow Coaching Advanced Coach Training Curriculum*

Patterson, James. "Assume nothing, question everything." *Cat and Mouse* (1997)

Herbert, Brian. "The capacity to learn is a gift; the ability to learn is a skill; the willingness to learn is a choice." *House Harkonnen* (2000)

Cohen, Leonard. "Forget your perfect offering. There is a crack in everything. That's how the light gets in." Song *Anthem* (1992)

Watts, Alan. "The only way to make sense out of change is to plunge into it, move with it, and join the dance." *The Wisdom of Insecurity: A Message for an Age of Anxiety* (1951)

Landers, Ann. "Some people believe holding on and hanging in there are signs of great strength. However, there are times when it takes much more strength to know when to let go and then do it." Syndicated Column (May 28, 1975)

Watts, Alan. "In the process of letting go, you will lose many things from the past, but you will find yourself." *The Wisdom of Insecurity: A Message for an Age of Anxiety* (1951)

The Movie, *Fallen*. "There are moments which mark your life, moments when you realize nothing will ever be the same and time is divided into two parts: before this and after this." (1998)

Chopra, Deepak. "One of the best things that you can do for yourself is to consciously notice the things you don't usually notice. It is a sign of great deep awareness to see what was obvious but was never noticed before." *The Book of Secrets: Unlocking the Hidden Dimensions of Your Life* (2004)

Foch, Ferdinand. "The most powerful force on earth is the human soul on fire. Tune out the noise and ignite yours." *Marshal Foch: His Own Words on Many Subjects* (1929)

Otto, Herbert. "Change and growth take place when a person has risked himself and dares to become involved with experimenting with his own life." *A Guide to Developing Your Potential* (1967)

Shedd, John A. "A ship in harbor is safe, but that is not what ships are built for." *Salt from My Attic* (1928)

Cite-Stream

On-Screen, On-Stage, On-Page

Sliding Doors romantic comedy (1998)

Groundhog Day an American fantasy comedy film (1993)

Jochen Wegner TED talk 2019 TED Summit in Edinburgh, Scotland: What happened when we paired up thousands of strangers to talk politics.
https://www.ted.com/talks/jochen_wegner_what_happen ed_when_we_paired_up_thousands_of_strangers_to_talk _politics

Brené Brown TED Talk 2010 TEDx Houston: The Power of Vulnerability
https://www.ted.com/talks/brene_brown_the_power_of_v ulnerability

Chimamanda Ngozi Adichie, TED Global 2009: The Danger of a Single Story
https://www.ted.com/talks/chimamanda_ngozi_adichie_th e_danger_of_a_single_story

Adam Kahane Book, *Solving Tough Problems* (2007)

Other Works by Donna Karlin

Leaders: Their Stories, Their Words: Conversations with Human-Based Leaders (Amazon, Kindle)

The Art of Addressing Situations in the Moment (Bookboon)

The Power of Coaching: Don't Give Up Your Day Job, or Should You? (Bookboon)

Submitted for Publication:

The Agile Mindset: Thriving in a fast-Changing Work Landscape—Bookboon

Breaking the Busy Trap: Flipping the Script on Productivity—Bookboon

Culture Catalyst: Igniting an Era of Inclusion, Innovation and Growth—Bookboon

Disruptive Collaboration: Unleashing the Power of Collective Intelligence—Bookboon

The Happiness Hacker's Guide to Business Domination—Bookboon

A League of Your Own: Discovering your Distinctive Advantage—Bookboon

The Intrapreneur's Manifesto: Challenging Conventions, Driving Change and Shaping the Future—Bookboon

The Power Persuasion Blueprint: Mastering Corporate Presentation Design—Bookboon

Radical Responsibility: Provocative Strategies for Ethical Leadership and Social Impact—Bookboon

Reverse Mentoring: Lessons from the New, For the Experienced—Bookboon

Team Alchemy: Cracking the Code of High-Performance Teams—Bookboon

The Resilient Mindset: Navigating Challenges and Thriving in a VUCA World—Bookboon